About the Author

Mike Delaney had a successful career as a nurse before reaching out and going into residential treatment for his addictions in 1996. He has since become a renowned mental health/addictions therapist, having developed and been CEO and the Clinical Director of several new treatment facilities as well as having a successful private practice in Harley Street, London. He is currently the Clinical Director of Delamere Health, the UK's first, purpose built, Addiction and Behavioural Health Clinic in Cheshire and is regularly asked for his expertise in newspapers, magazines and on television.

Behind the Smile

Mike Delaney

Behind the Smile

Olympia Publishers
London

www.olympiapublishers.com
OLYMPIA PAPERBACK EDITION

A CIP catalogue record for this title is
available from the British Library.

ISBN: 978-1-80074-407-3

First Published in 2023

Olympia Publishers
Tallis House
2 Tallis Street
London
EC4Y 0AB

Printed in Great Britain

Dedication

I dedicate this book to my daughter, Clare, and my grandchildren, Toni and Nevin, for their unconditional love and acceptance. xxx

Acknowledgements

Thank you to my family and friends for continuing to love me at a time when I couldn't love myself. A special thank you to Eileen and Chris for rescuing me from myself and holding me until I was strong enough to fly again. Thanks also to Michael Dunne for his friendship, loyalty and laughter over the last twenty-two years. A special thank you to my dear friend, Ann Mitchell, who took the time to sit with me, as a gifted and experienced actor, and to deconstruct a whole chapter in order that I could see a different and more authentic way to write, without fear or shame. 'I want to know exactly what that boy felt and what he did because of how he felt', Love you Ann. Gratitude is also felt for the fellowships of Alcoholics and Narcotics Anonymous who have provided amazing support over the years.

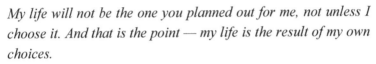

My life will not be the one you planned out for me, not unless I choose it. And that is the point — my life is the result of my own choices.
—Richelle E. Goodrich

Foreword

May you come to believe there is another way. May you find it now.
—Elizabeth Hearn

If nothing changes, nothing changes...

Mike's voluntary rehab encounter provided the frame for him to thrive emotionally, intellectually, spiritually and physically. With the support of counsellors, peers and the wider recovery community, over time, he recovered from his self-destructive relationship with alcohol and drugs, all the while developing the capacity for healthy interpersonal attachments, person-centred skills for sustaining autonomy, connection, continuing recovery and wellness.

Within the universal recovery community, many people's recovery may have begun with a moment of clarity. For others an intervention, at the right time and place. Mike's recovery began the moment he asked for help after a failed suicide attempt; a reoccurring dark night of the soul, embodying years of self-loathing, self-defeating behaviours, existential pain and suffering. The progression of Mike's addiction personified a self-sabotaging mindset, with the potency to convince him to end his suffering by suicide because he could not fix, forget or forgive himself for the consequences of any of his addictive behaviours.

Thankfully, there was another way waiting for him as soon as he became willing to accept help, and like many others before him, he has risen 'phoenix-like' from the ashes of active addiction.

Mike recounts his journey from abject fear to transformation, healing and hope. His words of wisdom are an invitation, to the reader, into his inner world. In addition to trusting wholeheartedly that his heartfelt message of healing and hope will be heard by anyone struggling to cope with complex trauma, addiction and mental health concerns, anxiety or depression.

Mike's intrinsic wisdom: that if he can recover, anyone who is continuing to suffer can begin to recover the moment they become willing to ask for help, and stop giving energy to self-defeating, self-stigmatising beliefs that they are helpless and hopeless, disenfranchised, disconnected, unworthy and unlovable human beings.

I am a person in long-term recovery – thirty-two plus years. Mike is an integral member of our shared universal recovery tribe, who continues to collectively and individually, walk the walk and talk the talk of freedom from physical cravings, obsession, compulsivity, distorted thinking and disconnection, defining, albeit negative traits at the heart of addiction experiences, which thankfully no longer have the power to sabotage and or diminish personal recovery.

"We have recovered. We keep coming back. We practice generosity of spirit by doing service within the recovery community. We are mindful of the value in maintaining openness, and compassion."

Mike is one of many in recovery who continues to enrich the lives of others.

Introduction

What doesn't kill you makes you stronger.

I have been toying with the idea of writing an honest account of my life for a few years now. I wrote a synopsis and a few basic chapters in 2008 but I didn't have the commitment to 'get it down' as I had a busy life and, at the time, the task seemed so huge. Apart from drugs and alcohol, my life was also fuelled by curiosity and excitement, so I have had a lot of different life experiences, some traumatic and some very happy. When I laid out the synopsis in chronological order, it was quite frightening to see the mountain that I would have to climb in order to write everything down and it was evident that I could not have fitted everything into one book. I suspect it would have been at least three books and would have taken me several years; so I felt that I had to come up with a concept which was different but which also gave detailed and powerful snapshots of my life.

I often think of myself as having lived two lives, often simultaneous, one which was carnage; filled with alcohol and drugs, and one filled with joy and success. I wanted to somehow combine the two but couldn't come up with a framework which held both extremes of my life. Then I had an idea.

In late 1996 I entered Broadway Lodge Treatment Centre in Weston-super-Mare following the most severe depression and suicidal period of my whole life, due completely to addiction to alcohol and drugs. I spent five months in that facility and it changed my life forever, showing me new strategies for living without the need for chemicals.

A huge part of this journey was taking an inventory of my life, the good, the bad and the ugly and understanding and taking responsibility for my behaviours. I thought that this therapeutic experience would be the perfect framework for my story and would allow me to choose the events which were significant for me to share, rather than documenting every single event. It will be written in the context of doing therapeutic assignment-work in treatment, but the examples will not necessarily be relevant to that experience at that time. This isn't my clinical step-work, it is a collection of experiences which I had to explore and address in treatment, but is written in a very different way in order to engage the reader

My book will begin at the very end of my addictive behaviour, when I didn't want to live another day on this planet. When I woke up every day and my eyes filled with tears because I was still alive and had to go through another day of torture. When I could hardly lift my head to say hello because my depression felt like a lead coat spread over my whole body. It will then chronicle my time in Broadway Lodge which will give insights into how the rehabilitation process works, but I will honestly share detailed major events in my life as I now understand them through 'flashbacks' as I did my Step Work in treatment. I hope that this idea will be interesting both for those with no experience of addiction and treatment, and for those who have travelled the same road as me and absolutely understand where I am coming from. Broadway was transformational and life changing for me and my second chance at life has been an amazing journey full of every emotion but ultimately it has been grounded in love and service.

Because of this style of writing, I am maintaining a certain level of confidentiality by not always using surnames and, in some instances, by changing names. This is in keeping with the Anonymous Recovery Fellowships rules of first name only, that is "my name is Mike and I'm an alcoholic."

I have also avoided flooding the book with the names of the many thousands of people whom I know through my work and travels. My friends know who they are and have been consistent throughout my life. They know how much I value and support their friendship, so I do not need to name them all to show this.

Due to issues of respect and privacy, there is an experience in my life which I will not be including in this book. I ask that the reader understands my reasons for this decision. For a number of years, I was married and settled with a stepfamily. I loved my wife and her children, and I tried to be a good husband and stepfather, however, addiction and depression were ever-present, and I was unable to be the man that they deserved. I was not difficult or aggressive, but, despite my best efforts, I was unable to be emotionally present for them. The decision to end the relationship was extremely difficult and painful to make, but I truly felt that my wife deserved much more than I could provide and deserved to be able to try again with someone who could meet her needs. I also knew that I had to continue to work on myself and avoid long term relationships and becoming enmeshed in other people's issues.

My life has been exciting, fun, scary, devastating, sad, difficult, unpredictable; but never dull. Although I have suffered trauma and pain, I am not only a survivor, but a thriver. My favourite thing is to laugh, to really laugh, and I make sure I do it every day. I love life with a passion and still look for new experiences and ways to enjoy myself. Although I was in active addiction for many years it didn't become unbearably painful until the last few years. Much of it was fantastic. I met wonderful and interesting people, and I was invited to some amazing parties and places. For a time, I truly 'lived on the edge' between two different lives which seldom met. One, as a healthcare professional, managing teams and caseloads, and one as a party-animal, frightened half to death but scared to miss an opportunity; so, I was always putting on a smile. Eventually it became too exhausting to continue, but for a while it was amazing!

This volume covers my journey into early recovery but there are several more volumes before I reach the present day.

I hope you enjoy my story.

—Mike

The Beginning of the End

We may encounter many defeats but we must not be defeated.
—Maya Angelou

It was the Summer of 1996, I was living in Wanstead, East London, and was managing a social services facility for adults with mental health and learning disabilities. Since my close friend Michael's death the previous year, I felt like a shadow, as if only part of me was actually there. I went through the motions of getting up and going to work every day but it felt like I was on automatic pilot. I didn't feel connected to anyone and I was clearly suffering from a severe depression, plus major traumas which had been layered through my experiences and losses in recent years.

Numb is too simplistic a word to describe what I was feeling. 'Like the walking dead' is probably a better metaphor. I could be dissociative for long periods, and simply stare into mid-air. I constantly swung between feeling acutely terrified and totally detached from life. My mind would not be still; it spoke to me constantly and not in a good way. It relentlessly told me how awful and pathetic I was and how much better everyone else would feel if I just fucked off and killed myself. The only thing preventing me from doing it was my job, I would have drunk myself to death if there was no reason not to. I had even convinced myself that my daughter would be relieved if I went because I was a crap dad anyway and kept letting her down.

There's no escape from ridicule if it's being supplied by you in your own head.

I sat in my little flat one night, having a few cans as I was working in the morning, listening to some of Michael's CDs when I became very low in my mood, but very clear in my thoughts. I made the decision that I would end my life the following day, and that would be it. I wouldn't have to suffer this agony and despair any longer; I could go and be with everyone that I had lost over the last decade. Almost immediately my mood lifted. I had found a solution and the reaction of my body had confirmed that it was the right one. I had little time to spare so I went to the off-licence and bought vodka and started to write my goodbye letters to the people closest to me. I tried to be honest in those letters, but they probably sounded psychotic and showed how disordered my thoughts were at that time. I finished my letters with a smile, sealed them all and laid them upright on my bedside table so that they could be found easily. I then continued to drink and turned my music up loud, because for the first time in a long time, I actually felt happy and excited about my plans.

Bright and early in the morning I showered and threw on shorts and a tee shirt. I nipped to Somerfield and bought six ready mixed gin-and-tonics, a bottle of vodka and six cans of Stella. My mood was somewhat elated as I began to plan my day and how I would shuffle off this mortal coil. After downing a few of my G+Ts in the little park across from the shops, I packed the remaining alcohol into my rucksack and headed for the tube as my plan involved West London. I sat on the Central Line drinking my cans and staring at the other passengers, almost praying that one of them would say something so that I could start a fight. Underneath my calm mood was a deep raging pool of anger which was driving my suicidal thoughts and feelings. "What are you fuckin' lookin' at?" I would bellow every so often, not caring who I was hurting or what the consequences might be. I no longer had to be a certain person, a professional, a son or a terrible dad. I could tell the whole world to fuck off!

I got off the train and on to the busy platform at Oxford Circus. It was still around ten thirty a.m. so there were still some commuters as well as the very many London tourists who spend hours looking at maps and trying to work out how to use the underground. 'Perfect' I thought to myself. 'This is the ideal place to jump in front of a train,' so I stood back for a few minutes drinking more Stella and started to decide when I should do it. My body and mind were determined that it was happening soon, so I stepped forward and stood on the yellow line. There were many people standing around me as I started to hear the rails vibrate and to see the light beginning to show in the tunnel as it came closer and, as I tensed my body to jump, a voice in my head said, 'You won't die, it will just cut your legs off!' I stepped back quickly as the front carriage thundered past and felt shocked at what had just happened. I sat on one of the benches and opened my vodka; took a long drink and tried to work out what the fuck was going on. Eventually I agreed with the voice, the thought of surviving and ending up in a wheelchair or in a care-home filled me with dread. I knew what to do, what would be a sure-fire success, so I left the station and went back up to the street and headed to Westminster Bridge. My anger was now spilling out on anyone who dared look at me, although inside I still felt insanely calm and determined that I would not be returning to my life. Ever.

I got to Westminster Bridge and, without looking, climbed up and swung my legs over the edge of the wall. I looked down to discover that the tide was out and all I could see directly beneath me was mud and stones! I filled my lungs to capacity and screamed, "Fuuuuucckkk!" at the top of my lungs because I knew the same thing would happen as with the train; I would break my ankles but survive. People were starting to approach, to see if I was ok, and I just kept shouting, "Fuck off and leave me alone!" as I headed back towards the parliament buildings.

I went back to Wanstead with a new plan and popped into my flat for my large 'Kitchen Devil' carving knife, then I collected my three-month prescription of anti-depressants and went back to Somerfield for more vodka and some newspapers and magazines to read whilst my plan progressed. Then I walked into Epping Forest. It was a beautiful sunny summers day, and I was very hot, so I hoped I could find a quiet space away from the sun and the families out walking. I walked along the public footpaths and then veered off hoping to find an isolated spot where I could end my life without being interrupted, or, found before I was dead and resuscitated by a passer-by. After a short time I found a shady thicket, where I had to break some branches to get into a covered clearing. It was like my own little private grassy igloo. Silent and totally secluded. Nobody would find me here unless I set fire to it!

I sat with my vodka, and with a couple of remaining cans, and slowly washed down a large quantity of my anti-depressants as I read about all the shit which was happening across the world. I could feel myself having 'absences' where my head would nod into a momentary unconsciousness. I knew I would have to cut my wrist soon or I would be unable to do it at all, so I reached into my rucksack and pulled out my knife.

There was an eerie silence, the sunlight was low in the shady place I had chosen. I swigged the last drop of vodka, screwed the lid back on and put it tidily back in my rucksack, picked the knife up and thought about what I had to do and how best I was going to do it. As my thoughts moved into intention, and I moved my right hand across to access my left wrist, I heard a crashing, breaking noise come from behind me and a huge German-Shepherd dog broke through the branches and came leaping over my head from behind, spun around on the ground in front of me, barked loudly and started licking my face! Again, I shouted, "For fuck's sake!" at the top of my voice as I dropped the knife to try and gain control over this mental dog!

"Major! Major! Come here!" I heard from the other side of the thicket. Major kept barking until his owner's head appeared through the space I had climbed through. "Oh, Major! There you are!" she said. Then as she suddenly realised there was a human under him she said in a surprised tone, "Are you OK?"

"I was fine until your fuckin' mutt came and interrupted me!" I replied in a slurred, shocked way.

"Oh I'm terribly sorry," she said. "Can I do anything to help you?" she said, as I felt the drugs and alcohol; like my courage, begin to rush out of my body as the shock had jolted me back to reality.

"I'm fine." I protested as I tried to get to my feet. I picked up my belongings and put them back in my rucksack in between being quizzed by her and licked to death by her dog. "I just forgot the time," I said as I climbed back out of my private space and tried to act as if everything was normal.

"Are you sure you're OK, love?" she persisted. I tried to be nice to her, but I was so angry that she had arrived and ruined my plan. I was so fed up with my plans being foiled.

"Listen!" I said, "Get yer dog and keep walking. Suffice to

say ye've ruined my plans but I'll be fine so just you forget you ever saw me!" She looked very upset and concerned for me when I couldn't muster a single bit of care or concern for myself. I walked slowly back to my flat with no feelings, no care, no idea what I was going to do. I looked around the room and wondered why I was still here and why everything was conspiring against me, but I had a final idea up my sleeve as I was truly at the very end of my rope.

I spent the next day planning my final attempt by sitting on my home phone telling those closest to me that I was doing a training course for a few days so wouldn't be at home. This way I could do it at home without being interrupted in the act, but would also be discovered in a few days. I then went out and procured more drugs and alcohol with the last bit of money I had. This had to work as I couldn't afford to live after today!

That evening was calm and considered. I played music which made me feel sorry for myself and which confirmed that I was a burden to everyone and would not be missed. I didn't cry or get emotional because my disordered thinking had convinced me that it was the only way, that I had no choice. It was like a transaction; once I did the final deed everything would go back to normal for everyone else. Yes, they may cry a few tears initially, but very quickly they would say, 'it was a blessing', and their lives would be complete again. I remember this in detail because my thoughts were so strong and sure of themselves, I didn't argue.

Again, after copious amounts of alcohol and prescription drugs I was falling into unconsciousness and decided it was time. I was in my bed wearing only a tee shirt and shorts and had the knife on my bedside table. I checked that the goodbye letters were in view and picked up the knife. I remember meticulously inserting the point of the knife into my wrist and turning it before pulling it towards me. Painless, but I felt the blood starting to pour, so dropped the knife to the floor and turned the lamp off so that I couldn't see and distress myself. I lay back on my pillow and felt myself losing consciousness, and I felt relief. No more pain. No more trauma. I started to pray in my head, I called for Michael in the darkness of my room. "I'll be there with you soon," I said confidently as I drifted into oblivion. I could feel myself smiling for the first time in a long time because it was over.

I started to see a light as I emerged from the warmth and calmness of my last conscious memories, but I very quickly realised that I was not in heaven, I was still in my bed and still alive. I felt my eyes fill with tears. How could I possibly still be here? I felt a sharp stabbing pain and looked down to see my left arm stuck to my tee shirt with a load of clotted blood which was also all over the bed and floor. I must have rolled over onto my arm, unconscious, and stopped the bleeding. I sat up, on the side of the bed, with my left arm attached and facing upwards as if I was wearing a sling. I was so angry in that moment I could have screamed but it would have drawn attention from my neighbours. I wasn't consciously crying but tears were flowing from my eyes in buckets. I didn't know what to do next; I'd exhausted every plan, also my bank account was now empty, and I hadn't planned for today, so I didn't know what to do. Being the one who always looked after others I didn't know how to look after myself. For the first time in my life, I was going to have to admit defeat and ask for help. The thought filled me with horror; but I had nothing left, nowhere left to go. I couldn't speak. I couldn't think straight. Someone would have to take over as I had nothing left.

I picked up my phone and dialled my sister Eileen's number.

"Hello" came the familiar, safe voice.

"Hiya, hen," I said in a slow, quiet tone.

"Is that you, Michael?" she replied, "I thought you were on a course?"

"I've done something stupid, Eileen, and I don't know what to do. I'm really sorry hen but I don't know what to do," I said, feeling ashamed of asking my little sister to help me out. "I've tried to kill myself," I said in a matter-of-fact tone.

"What?" said Eileen. "Are ye ok?"

"I'm ok," I replied. "But I don't know what to do. I've never felt like this before, so I don't know how to get out of it." We arranged to meet in a pub in Wanstead so I cleaned myself up a bit, bound a dressing and a crepe bandage around my wrist and left the blood-soaked carnage behind me.

When I got to the pub Eileen and Chris were sitting at a table, Chris got up and asked what I wanted to drink. "Sorry Chris, I don't really want a drink but I will have to drink as my body is going into withdrawal." I sat down next to Eileen, feeling emotionless and detached, as if I was in a different time-zone. I could see the shock on her face which made me feel worse. "I'm sorry, hen, I didn't know what to do and didn't want to get you involved but I just couldn't go on like this any longer; I still don't want to be here, but for the moment, I am." I could see my words cause both Chris and Eileen pain, so I went silent and tried to drink some lager without spilling it because I was shaking so much.

"Michael, I never knew it was this bad; you should have said something," said Eileen, trying to make sense of everything.

I couldn't think of the words to reply. I couldn't think about anything really. I didn't continue the conversation as I had nothing to say. I answered any questions they asked but it was the hardest work I had ever done to engage and talk. I didn't want to be here anymore, but I was stuck here; I was like a prisoner who'd been refused parole after years of punishment. "You need to come back and stay with us in Loughton." They both agreed. "We'll find some help for you on Monday. Do you want to go back and pick anything up?" asked Eileen.

"No," I replied, "I don't want to go back in there at the moment, it's a terrible mess."

"OK," said Eileen. "Just come back with us and Chris or I can pop in tomorrow and pick some stuff up. We'll stop at a supermarket and get some drink in for you so you don't get ill, and we will make a plan from there." I nodded my head and was very grateful that they were trying to help me, but I felt nothing. I had a depression which was blocking everything positive from coming in or going out to help me.

We arrived in Loughton and Eileen ran me a hot lavender bath and gave me a cuddle. "Just lie in there for a wee while, the lavender will help you relax."

"Thanks, hen," I said as I locked the door and took off my shorts and tee-shirt. I looked at my naked emaciated body in the mirror and wondered how it had come to this. How had I been so strong for so long and now I probably weighed around six or seven stones with not an ounce of strength left in me. I lay in the bath and breathed in the lavender, hoping that I would feel some benefit from it, but my body felt like it had shut down and was not letting anything in.

A few days later Eileen drove me to an appointment in Romford with a drug and alcohol service. I had a full assessment and due to my continued depression and suicidal ideation they agreed to fund a three week detox in a clinic called Rugby House in Central London. I thanked them for their support and a day or two later I got the tube to Holborn to start my detox. Rugby House was a nicely decorated building with keyworkers, and group therapy, and educational sessions as part of the programme, but it was detox-only so not too much commitment needed. They had some very good staff but the focus of everyone in treatment and the most popular person in the building was the chef; a West Indian lady called Janet who fed everyone until they were back to health. It was an open-plan kitchen, so she was always part of the patient group as her kitchen was attached to our seating area.

The smells from her cooking were continual, and she was always sitting encouraging people to eat. I loved her attitude and some of my first smiles were caused by her unrelenting care and concern for the residents. Another life-changing moment came when I was coerced into attending an AA meeting which was held nearby. I sat in the meeting, judging everything that I heard and finding every reason why they were different from me, when I suddenly felt the urge to say, for the first time, "My name is Mike and I'm an alcoholic." The large group sat listening, so I then briefly explained that I didn't know why I was here or why I felt the need to speak and that I had tried to kill myself a short time ago (I still had dressings on my arm). At the end of the meeting which I thought was boring and not something I wanted to engage with, an older Irish lady, who had shared earlier, approached me in my seat and asked if she could have a word with me. "Thank you for your honesty when you shared Michael," she said in a strong Irish accent and using my full name, before leaning over and cupping my face in her hands. "The reason you are still here is that God has a plan for you. You just don't know what it is yet." For some reason her words and actions touched me deeply and I began to cry. She wiped my tears and kissed my forehead. "Keep coming back and you might just find out what it is," she said as she squeezed my arm and headed out of the building. I have never forgotten that moment as something inside of me shifted at that point. I still felt ashamed and depressed and angry and sad, but I didn't want to die.

My 'Sober Birthday' is 30 September 1996 which occurred whilst I was in Rugby House. After three weeks of treatment and initially intending to go straight back to work I suddenly thought about the enormity of my situation and decided that I should fight for a rehab place and make an effort to get well.

I tried every which way to get funding from my employers, from the drug and alcohol service and from some charitable organisations but it was tough. I was still staying at Eileen's and going out every day to meetings and trying to find someone to fund me. Eventually, almost three months later and miraculously, still sober, I was granted part funding from the drug and alcohol service and I was assessed and offered a place at Broadway Lodge in Weston-super-Mare. My life was about to change forever.

'You learn more from failure than from success. Don't let it stop you. Failure builds character.'
—Anonymous

My arrival in rehab

After several months of 'blowing in the wind' trying to stay clean and sober since my three week detoxification in London in September 1996, I was eventually granted part-funding for my rehabilitation at Broadway Lodge. My keyworker in London felt that this would be a good option for me, so I trusted his advice and agreed to travel down to Weston for an eight week residential programme.

Broadway Lodge stands imposingly on a hill overlooking the Oldmixon area of Weston-super-Mare. Formerly a hunting lodge, then a convent, before becoming the UK's first, Minnesota model treatment centre around 1974; the building was very grand with beautiful original features such as the stunning entrance staircase and stained-glass windows depicting hunting scenes from days gone by. It was surrounded by beautifully maintained gardens with various levels, seating areas and a large pond which was useful for contemplating the next step when one felt like giving up the fight to get well and return to their old ways! My brother-in-law Chris had driven me down from London in November 1996 and, after a quick cup of tea, he was quickly bundled out of the front door and I was left alone to take the next frightening step of my journey.

Initially I was shown into a large lounge with a huge bay-window which looked out over Weston, an ever-changing landscape of built-up housing estates and countryside. The lounge was full of patients huddled in groups, smoking, chatting and talking about their feelings! I remember thinking, 'Oh my God, what have I done?' when people began to approach me and introduce themselves and, a bit like prison movies, asked, "What are you in for?" Some of them looked and sounded very healthy, whilst others looked frail and vulnerable; shaking as they tried to drink their tea or coffee. There were quiet people and loud people, funny people and very serious people. One of the first things I noticed however, was the atmosphere, the energy of the building, which was happy and warm and friendly, but most of all it felt safe. It had been quite a long time since I had felt any sense of safety, acceptance or belonging so it was a bit of a shock to feel people's concern for me; to sit down and hear a bit about their journey and to get hugged! So many hugs!

There were around thirty patients in 'Primary Care' at that point and we were divided into three groups for our twice daily therapy sessions. It was a mixture of addictions, mainly Alcohol or Heroin but also a few eating disordered patients who also worked the twelve-step programme. At 'the bottom of the garden' was extended care where some people went after primary to gain more skills and confidence before returning to their lives outside. I knew I only had 8 weeks to get my shit together before returning to work and family so, at that point, I didn't think about the possibility, or indeed the need for extended care.

I was pretty sure I could master this in eight weeks and be 'cured' from this condition which had plagued me for twenty years. How naïve I was to believe that when I hadn't yet been 'unpicked' or 'unpacked' by my peers or counsellors, so I therefore had no idea what was about to happen to me or what actually underpinned and fed all of my addictive processes.

The patients had very basically divided the population of the building into 'smack-heads', 'red-noses' and 'foodies'. As I didn't understand the treatment process at this time I was initially very compliant and 'nice' to everyone who spoke to me. This would change once I understood self-worth, honesty and my 'caretaking' behaviours associated with co-dependency. After a short time, I was called to the Medical Department for the 'Admission' which was very formal and detailed. A polaroid mug-shot was taken for identification purposes and a full history and progression of addiction was also taken. I felt lucky that I had already detoxed so didn't have to go through that discomfort again and I felt more able to hit the ground running and do the work I needed to do. Then there was a full medical examination by a doctor followed by another torrent of questions about what I had done and with whom, before I was officially a patient and was able to return to the lounge area.

I was then introduced to my 'Buddy' a young Birmingham lad called Steve who was in for heroin addiction and who was doing very well. He showed me around the building; dining room, bedrooms, showers, lecture hall and explained the very strict rules and the consequences if these were broken. He explained the mealtimes and that you had to attend, even if you didn't want to eat. The timetable of lectures, groups and other sessions and that they were also compulsory, and had to be attended for fear of consequence. He also explained the peer-support system which included group-leaders and a house-leader whose responsibility it was to ensure that the system was running as it should and to report any issues to the staff when it wasn't. This was a great way of gently giving responsibility back to people who had avoided it for so long and who were frightened by 'real life'. One of the features that stood out was the bell. One of the House-Leaders duties was to ring an old school hand bell, at the start of every activity throughout the day. Seven-thirty wake up, eight breakfast, nine-fifteen morning lecture. We were like a group of Pavlov's dogs jumping to attention every time the bell rang!

At that time in 1996, the requirements for single occupancy rooms and en-suite bathrooms hadn't yet been established, so I found myself sharing a six-bedded dormitory-style room with 5 other males with a variety of ages and personalities from different parts of the country. I must admit to feeling very anxious about sharing 'private space' with so many strangers and feeling deeply disappointed that I didn't get a single room, en-suite and my own personal butler, but unbeknown to me, my delusions of grandeur were about to be smashed into a million little pieces.

All of my beliefs which I clung on to in order to believe that I wasn't as bad as everybody else were systematically dismantled, sometimes gently, sometimes brutally, but they were destroyed, and I came to understand that I was no better or worse than anyone else and that we were all in this place because we all had the same problem: addiction. It didn't matter if you were a nurse, like me, or you were a burglar who was stealing to feed his habit, or you were a high court judge who was caught drink-driving.

We had all come to a point where we could no longer continue managing our lives in the way we had been, hence the powerful wording of Step One:

We admitted we were powerless over our addiction, that our lives had become unmanageable.

I can still remember reading those words for the first time and allowing the meaning to permeate the hard, defensive shell which I had created to protect myself. One of the most powerful words which hit me like a train was very simply 'we', I had felt ashamed, frightened and alone for what seemed like such a long time that knowing others understood exactly how I felt and had travelled the same horrific road as me was overwhelming. I remember actually breaking down and sobbing at the simplicity and strength of those words. I was no longer alone.

I remember my first evening meal in Broadway, feeling anxious about not making any gaffes or sitting at the wrong table or doing something that someone else could pull me up on but I needn't have worried. The meal started with a meditation being read out by a member of the group then, what felt like a feast was served out from the middle of each table. Beautifully cooked food, presented so well and it tasted like nothing else I had ever tasted. When you've been addicted to substances and smoked for a long time, your taste buds become dulled and unresponsive. Well I think my taste buds woke up all at once when I had my first meal at Broadway. Not only was the food wonderful but the noise of chatter and so much laughter amidst so much pain was astonishing to me. The quick-witted humour and unbelievable stories that poured out during meals were a tonic for the soul. In no time I was joining in and laughing uncontrollably for the first time in years. I was beginning to feel less different and more connected to everyone in the building. I felt shocked and guilty for having so much fun, like I didn't deserve to laugh or enjoy life, but the coming weeks were to show me exactly why I carried these feelings and the huge part that shame played in my upbringing and subsequent addictions.

As I hadn't yet seen my counsellor or been given any assignment work, my first evening was spent simply talking and sharing in the lounge, being approached at various times by various patients. Some who were shy and couldn't greet me when I was with a group, some who were curious about my story and some just genuinely wanted to make sure I was OK. I still smoked at that time, so every cigarette was a conversation with another person or a group of people.

After a light supper at around ten-thirty it was lights-out. It was to be my first night in a large, packed bedroom with people I was only just getting to know. Although apprehensive, I acted 'as if' and climbed the old staircase to my room. I look back now and wonder why I was ever concerned because bedtime was to become the liveliest and funniest part of the day by far! Once everyone was in bed, the jokes and funny conversations started as none of us were used to going to sleep without alcohol or drugs. Things that had happened during the day would be revisited and re-framed in humorous ways. The staff would all be impersonated by my room-mates who had their voices and body language down to a tee. It was like re-visiting my childhood every night and being told-off and scolded by night staff for making a noise which automatically made us worse. Sometimes I could not catch my breath as some of my peers were so funny with rapid-fire jokes.

'It's not whether you get knocked down, it's whether you get back up.'
—Vince Lombardi

Settling in.

Settling-in to Broadway wasn't too difficult as I liked the majority of the other patients who were sharing the experience with me. There were a couple of people whom I avoided because I just didn't like their attitude or arrogance. My understanding of human behaviour is better now, and I realise that the loudness and arrogance comes from a place of low self-esteem and confidence and is a defence to prevent others seeing that vulnerable part of you.

Most of the group were just getting through by doing the best they could. The lounge was a melting pot of emotions; vulnerability, support and most of all laughter. We were all in so much pain because of the work we were doing that laughter became the default setting to cope with it. As a nurse I was well used to this strategy as it was commonplace within mental health services.

Back then the pub became the processing point for the different experiences of my day; and they were often very difficult and at times traumatic events. I remember in my early days as a community psychiatric nurse, before lone working policies and safe working policies were introduced, I was asked by my team psychiatrist if I would go down to the thatched house area of Leytonstone to 'visit a young man who is having some difficulty with his mother'. The mother had rung us to say he was being aggressive and she was concerned that he had stopped taking his medication. I had said, "No problem." As was the way back then and arrived at the terraced house on Cann Hall Rd 37.

The door was opened slightly by a young male who said suspiciously, "What do you want?" I informed him who I was and that his mother had called as she was concerned about him. "You better come in," he said as he opened the door and indicated for me to enter. As I passed him moving into the hall I turned around to ask which room to go into and realised he was holding a twelve-inch carving knife in his hand!

Trying not to react and make the situation worse I said, "Is there somewhere we can sit and have a chat?"

To which he meekly replied, "In there." He nodded his head in the direction of the lounge. As I walked towards the room I noticed that another door to a bedroom had six inch nails hammered chaotically into the frame, holding it shut and from the muffled noises I guessed that his mother was inside.

I sat on an armchair, expecting him to sit on the sofa opposite, however he sat on the floor right in front of my feet and, although agitated and upset, he was not threatening me so I decided to engage in dialogue and see if I could get us all out of the situation safely. I asked him why he was feeling the way he was and he described a difficult morning with his religious mother, as she wanted him to go to a special Church service and he didn't want to go. He then became agitated describing what she had been saying and how pressured he felt; as he spoke he had started to stab the carpet in front of him with the knife.

Again, he hadn't been intending to frighten me, he was releasing his anger through his actions. I empathised with him and assured him that he wasn't in trouble and that I wouldn't be informing the police, however I did suggest that I could help him to get some space by taking him into hospital for some respite care and treatment. He nodded in agreement but continued to retell the story of his day.

By this time the carpet around him was shredded and there were splinters of wood from the floorboards beginning to join the carpet shreds. His energy begun to dip and he began to cry rather than continue being angry. He was remorseful and upset at what he had done and realised that it was not his normal behaviour to do this type of thing. He was also eager that I should not think badly of him and I assured him that I was actually very impressed at the way he had settled down and shared his experience.

I smiled at him and said, "Shall we get your mum out of the room and check that she is OK?" He responded quickly, as if he had forgotten what he had done.

"Oh, yes please, can you help me…" We got a claw hammer from the kitchen and managed to get the bedroom door open to find his mum quite calm and relieved that everything was under control. I introduced myself and said that I was going to take her son into hospital for a little while to assess him and review his meds.

He looked at me suddenly with a shocked expression, but I spoke calmly and said, "Remember we spoke and you agreed that you needed a break away from this house?" He nodded his head in agreement. I asked him to pack a few things while I checked on his mum who insisted that she was just a bit shaken as she had 'been here before'. Within the hour I had called for back-up from their house phone (there being no mobiles in 1987!) and we transported him to hospital successfully. There was no 'well done' or 'good work' or any formal support framework for de-briefing, so, on many occasions I was just left to carry all of the emotional fallout and trauma from a normal day.

There was no supervision or support so every night in the pub became the place where I met colleagues from nursing and social work teams who were experiencing the same risky situations as me and we would 'put the world to right, offload our frustrations and once again begin to laugh. It wasn't a formal group but it was all we had and the situation I've described is just one of many which made the job very dangerous at times. The only difference between me and my colleagues was that they were not addicted and did not feel the need to drink every night whereas I did. I was first into the pub at five p.m. and last out at eleven-thirty p.m. every night.

Memories like that were emerging thick and fast during my treatment. When I first arrived and was asked to do different assignments I would protest and say, "I can't remember that! It was years ago, and I was drinking so I have no memory!" However, when you sit down and start to access old memories, it's as if a vault has been opened and, at some points, my hand was writing quicker than my mind could process what was coming through. Sometimes I felt as if I was 'channelling' the memories and not consciously in control of my actions.

As I moved forward and, for the first time, started to understand my processes and why I did certain things, I had to face the fact that many of my childhood needs were unmet. I do not say that with any blame or shame attached, rather with understanding and some admiration for what was achieved with so little. By this I mean my parents had eight young children to feed and clothe from one meagre labourer's salary. There was no benefit system to speak of back then. I remember as a young boy, accompanying my mum to the National Assistance office as my dad had lost his job and she had no income at all. I can still remember the dark smoky room in Falkirk where desperate people avoided eye contact from the shame of being in their position. I think the amount that was granted her was truly minimal and I remember her crying as we left, she then headed straight for the pawn shop to sell her silver tea service which they had received as a wedding gift. As it turned out it was silver plated so was worth very little and we left the shop with another paltry amount.

The '60s were a very tough time for poor families and the housing scheme where I lived had a good number of large Catholic families, because birth control was not allowed so many women seemed to be permanently pregnant. One thing I can honestly say about my family's situation is that, despite periods of extreme hardship, we never went hungry, and, by that I mean that my mum was a genius at making a small amount of meat or fish go very far. "It's like the bliddy loaves and the fishes in this hoose!" she would say as she spooned out stovies or stew or ham soup to our family; plus any relatives who were visiting and any of our friends who happened to be in the house. She would never see a child without food whilst we ate and would always stretch whatever was on the menu, to include them. Her food was also wholesome and filling which many Irish descendants were expert at preparing as they had learned from their starving forefathers. "I'm constantly robbing Peter to pay Paul!" was another of my mum's descriptions of how she could juggle a minimal amount of money in order to get maximum benefit from it. She ran a Kays Catalogue for years and many relatives and friends bought from her. She could then collect 'club money' from them and this would tide her over until Dad's wages came in when she would pay it back. In recovery I have sat and tried to work out how she managed to do what she achieved financially, and I just cannot. It was like a miracle.

The negative side of our family life as children was accepting that we couldn't have what other people had in terms of nice clothes, holidays, possessions. We did have quite extravagant Christmas presents (most of which came from the catalogue), but we didn't get many other gifts over the year and we usually only got a new set of clothes for the Annual Gala. The stress my parents were under must have been extraordinary but, so often, we children received the brunt of it. Physical punishment was commonplace back then and our family were particularly adept at it. We didn't get the odd slap on the back of the legs or a spanked bottom, we were beaten quite severely at times, depending on how much the adult happened to lose control. Picking up an object to assist with that was also a common way to ensure that the punishment was felt.

When I say many of my childhood needs were unmet, I really mean at an emotional level; important needs like feeling loved and nurtured, valued and heard were areas where my experience was lacking. Shame was a weapon that was used in every aspect of my life, from parents, schoolteachers, priests and anyone else who was older and knew who you were. I was often slapped by complete strangers for giggling in Church or in the streets. 'Children should be seen and not heard' was the mantra of the day and woe betide you if you broke that rule when a visiting priest or other guest was in the house. Having said that, I became an argumentative, cheeky child as I had to survive in a cut-throat family system. Last to the table, worst fed. Last up in the morning, worst dressed in school. Having a sharp mind and the ability to make adults laugh saved my hide many times!

My first proper assignment from my counsellor was to write my life-story, a detailed account of my childhood, adolescence, family system, relationships, career etc. It felt like a huge piece of work but, as I began to remember things, I found a pace and a flow.

Life Story

Don't worry what others are doing. Do you!
—Russell Simmons

When most people are in the throes of their detox regime and feeling like shit, they are introduced to their counsellor and given their life-story assignment which is a way of letting your peers get to know you a bit better, but also a way of building a timeline of your life and identifying any difficult or traumatic events. I tried to make my life-story positive and happy, but having been born into a large family only fifteen years after the end of World War Two, life was tough. This is a summary of my life-story up until my teenage years:

Dad wasn't around much when I was a child as he was always working shifts. Mum was having babies and 'robbing Peter to pay Paul', trying to balance very little finance and bring up eight children. I remember some happy times; laughter, singing, parties and I can also remember unhappy times; arguing and fighting in the house, drunk strangers wandering into the bedrooms looking for the toilet.

One thing I can remember clearly was a complete love and reliance on my brother John who was two years younger than me; although we felt like twins as we were inseparable. My mum usually dressed us the same and we shared one bunk bed and one life for many years. Sadly, puberty broke the dependence as I began to enjoy some of the pleasures of growing up and he was still at school. We did form a band for a few years and John was a major driving force in this. He studied lead guitar and quickly became an accomplished guitarist. Whilst myself Brian and Pat were working full time and going out drinking, John was focused, and spent most of his time practicing guitar or piano. To this day he is a very talented and gifted musician.

I can remember starting school at St Patrick's in 1965 and my first day in 'The Babies.' My earliest memories are of wooden floors, the smell of wood polish and sawdust, school dinners, the playground with the rounders pitch painted on the tarmac, windows which opened by pulling a cord, milk being delivered to each classroom on a trolley by Mr McNeill the Janitor, wellington boots, pink custard, Janet and John, The Wishing Chair. My first teacher was a Mrs Simpson, who was very gentle and well spoken, possibly English. I remember being surrounded by varying degrees of chaos: children screaming, children pissing and shitting themselves, children crying for their mums and dads. There were small tables and chairs, a sand pit, drawing paper and chubby stump crayons and a library of picture books. I seem to remember we were in the main hall with the little stage. There were around thirty kids in my class. I don't remember feeling scared or crying for anyone or even wanting to leave, however I remember feeling jealous when everyone else's mothers came to pick them up at home-time and I was picked up by my brother Andrew who was in an older class.

The school was an old-fashioned single storey, grey roughcast building in the shape of a Celtic Cross with a variety of wooden extensions and annexes added on as the catholic population of the town increased. It was surrounded by playing fields and mature trees which were perfect for climbing if you were that way inclined. The site was completely surrounded by a spiked perimeter fence made of black wrought iron with two separate gated entrances. Directly across the small road leading from the school to the main street stood St Alexander's, the only Catholic Church in the town which, at that time, was an extremely busy and well used facility with three halls attached for various children's and adult's clubs. I absolutely loved my seven years at St Patrick's R.C. Primary School. It was at a time when teachers were truly inspirational and could hold the attention of thirty children with a few words. Where thirty children would sit quietly and attentively, awaiting the next word. Where teachers knew parents and siblings and would enquire about them. Where special women like Mrs Mc Peake, Mrs Lopinska and Mrs McAlister would inspire us to learn, to behave well and to become good people.

It was around the age of six or seven, whilst in the playground of St Patrick's that I first recall being called sissy, a word whose connotations would come to haunt me. I had absolutely no earthly idea what it meant, and I remember defending myself, saying, "I'm not a sissy!" But of course, the perpetrator was fuelled by the reaction and the inevitable chanting of 'yes, you are!' and 'no, I'm not!' would go on forever! It was several years before I fully understood what the insult meant, let alone realised that it was actually true. Everyone except me knew that I was gay a long time before I was even remotely aware of its meaning. The words 'jessie', 'sissy' and 'poof' were hurled at me on a daily basis both in and out of school over the next ten years and, as I reached adolescence and its usage became more and more intense and hateful, it began to hurt deeply and I began to nurture a sense of profound shame about who I was even though I didn't know who I was. I just knew that people didn't like it so it must be wrong. Despite these feelings I had acceptance among my close friends and they were very careful in their avoidance of the words which they knew would hurt me, although the topic of my sexuality was never discussed until many years later.

Throughout my childhood, my family, as with most large families of that time, could be either supportive or abusive depending on the general atmosphere of the day. If it was a good day in the household, I could have fun and feel special through making people laugh. On another day I could be told to "Get to fuck ya little cunt!" by the same people who were laughing their heads off earlier. My family lived in a council housing scheme which was commonly known back then as Fenian Alley as there were so many catholic families living there. Our house was what is called a Scotch House in other parts of the country, namely one building divided into four flats of equal size, two up and two down. We were in the downstairs right side flat and had back and front doors and gardens. My grandfather was next-door, and the two upstairs flats were also occupied by large catholic families, The McNallys and The McCaffertys, later to be The Mitchells, not to mention other families scattered around the neighbouring roads, so the streets around my house were always full of children playing a multitude of games from kick-the-can to chap-door-run or 'chappie' as we preferred to call it. Most of this period in the '60s was sound-tracked by the music of The Beatles, The Rolling Stones, Cilla Black, Dusty Springfield and the sounds of Tamla Motown. Music was a major positive part of our family life whether it was singing at parties, learning the latest pop songs or just listening to 45's on our Dansette record player with the gold knobs. Music eased some of the pain and made life more bearable. It was a very effective escape from the madness of life in a large catholic family!

One of my favourite songs from that period was 'Band of Gold' by Freda Payne. I could lose myself in the music and forget reality. Every night after school I used to do 'the messages' for my Aunt Janet who worked as a night-nurse. I had developed a trusting relationship with her, and she wasn't too observant about prices or the correct change, so this became my first experience of scamming money. I could always pocket a few shillings and manage to cover it up. With my booty I would go to the back room in the Assu-Mar Café at Denny Cross. I would order a plate of chips, a Coke and would then fill the juke box with my remaining money, playing 'Band of Gold' and other hits of the day. I loved being out of the house and dreamed about growing up and moving away. Having become somewhat over-confident and a bit complacent around scamming the money from Aunt Janet, I made a big mistake one day when trying to dispose of my ill-gotten gains. I went to the pet-shop and bought a rabbit which cost 12 shillings and sixpence, around 62.5 pence in today's money. This was a huge amount of money for a child to have at that time and the first question snarled at me when I got home with a large black and white rabbit in a box was "Where the hell did ye get the money for that?" My acting abilities were in their infancy then, however I managed to pull the face of an altar boy and said indignantly, "I've been saving for that rabbit for weeks!" To my absolute shock it worked and no more questions were asked! That altar boy face went on to save me a million times!

The living situation in a three-bedroomed flat was crowded to say the least. Mum and Dad had one room, Alice, Eileen and Judith had another and Luke, Duncan, Andrew, John and I had the third. With five boys sharing one room there was always a variety of odours present at any given time, but predominantly it was rancid feet. The carpet was rarely visible because of all the discarded clothing, shoes, wellingtons, broken toys, jackets coats and anything else which didn't easily hang from the doorknob on the lobby press. The house décor was typical of the time, orange fibre-glass curtains, purple patterned wallpapers mixed with some remaining utility furniture. Despite the constant efforts of my mum to keep the house decorated, it was like the Forth Road Bridge, and with the constant human traffic seven days per week, it never looked fresh for long. Footballs, roller skates, bikes, prams and a million other pieces of junk were dragged in and out of the house, along the lobby and into the bedrooms, tearing wallpaper and marking floors and paintwork. As you can imagine, with only one bathroom and toilet, privacy was never an option in our house. The only time when you could expect to be left alone was when sitting on the toilet and even then, there was a constant knocking on the door followed by, "Who's in?", "Hurry up, I'm bursting!" and "If you don't get a move on, I'll kick the door in!" However, despite the interruptions, the toilet became a haven where I could think about things, where I could sit and read, and it became the room where I learned to cry in silence.

I was always very in touch with my emotions, not screaming hysterical I might add, just emotional. My responses to people were always empathic and even at a very young age I could feel sadness deeply and cry when others were suffering. I dreaded films like Lassie Come Home as, unlike my brothers, I couldn't hide my emotions and would find myself weeping uncontrollably whilst everyone else pointed and laughed in a bid to avoid their own tears. One such film was Imitations of Life with Lana Turner. The story was one of racism, and the rejection of a poor black mother by her wealthy and successful, apparently white, daughter. In the final scenes the mother dies and during her funeral procession, her daughter's feelings of guilt and shame about her treatment of her mother erupt and she chases the carriage carrying the coffin, screaming hysterically, apologizing and declaring her love. At around ten years old, I found this scene unbearable. In a bid to calm down, I walked to the chip shop with my brother John and my cousin Frances, but I could not stop crying for the rejected mother. I was absolutely in touch with the fact that I was different from the rest of my family, from my peers, from what was seen as normal within my society and that if I did not alter who I was, I would be rejected too. The fear of that rejection haunted me.

Next door to my house lived my grandfather, a retired miner and ex-wrestler who had suffered a number of heart attacks and strokes over the years. He had a very hard life and lost his wife, my grandmother, when his four daughters and one son were still young. Although he remarried some years later his new wife also died, so my mum, Aunt Alice Mary, Aunt Frances, Aunt Margaret and Uncle Michael had never really had a stable mother figure in their lives. They absolutely adored their father and looked after him for many years. With no mother around, they had been brought up by a selection of aunts in the days when open affection was less common; when you brushed yourself down and got on with it, where grief and sadness were luxuries you just couldn't afford. The elderly women in the family like Aunt Sal seemed to be quite hardened by their own pain and could not easily show their feelings to others, however in many ways their survival skills were admirable. They survived two world wars and were often widowed, bringing up large families single-handedly in the days before benefits.

My Auntie Lizzie was one such lady, she was widowed at a

young age with four children and had to go out most nights and play the piano in pubs and clubs and at weekends, play for weddings and concert parties. Her and my Auntie Bell were infamous and inseparable and, even in their later years could be heard screaming and laughing like teenagers! Auntie Lizzie had a one-liner for every occasion and wasn't afraid to use them. I remember one day my sister Alice, coming into the sitting room and, walking over to the window to see if her friends had arrived yet. It was the late '60s and, as a fashion-conscious teenager, she was wearing a mini skirt. Before she had a chance to say a single word, Auntie Lizzie bellowed, "If that skirt wiz any shorter ye'd have to take a hem up on yer knickers!" Golden memories.

My granda' was a beautiful man. Strong and determined, yet gentle and loving, he was fiercely proud of and protective of his family. The severity of his strokes had badly affected his speech and his ability to control his swallowing reflex. This caused him the most severe embarrassment as he choked on his food and drinks daily, but he never gave up trying and he always maintained the highest level of dignity in spite of his disabilities. His method of showing love and affection was to wrestle and play fight when his grandchildren visited. He would suddenly grab us, put us in a head lock and tickle until we submitted. This would make both him and us laugh and I imagine gave him a feeling of being connected to us in a non-verbal way. He would also make every effort to attend any concerts or shows which we might be in, such as the annual St Patrick's Night concerts. He would sit near the front and would watch intently to ensure that none of us forgot the words. I can still see him sitting there, staring up at me with a smile on his face whilst I sang 'If You're Irish, Come into the Parlour' with the rest of Mrs Dunnigan's choir. When he finally died in 1976, the year my nursing career began, a bright light went out within our family and it was never the same again.

Aunt Alice-Mary lived with Granda' and had taken over the matriarchal role soon after the death of her mother. Aunt Margaret and her two sons Duncan and Michael also lived there, as did Uncle Dan, a disabled World War One veteran until his death when I was six. His was the first dead body I ever saw and was my first experience of grief and loss although I don't remember being upset by it all. I thought his corpse looked very funny as his dentures seemed to be protruding from his mouth, then I went back to playing hide and seek in the street. As a child I witnessed lots of care and love within that house. Two adults with severe disabilities were looked after until their death with no question of hospitals or care homes and they were made to feel loved and wanted. Aunt Alice-Mary was a major source of love, support and affection within our family. She loved children. She listened to us and spent time with us. She bought us presents and was demonstrative in her love; a quality which was so rare at that time. When she married Uncle John, my dad's brother, and moved out of my granda's house I missed her greatly, even though she visited every day to make his dinner etc. It wasn't too long before she managed to get a house across the street, where she lived with Uncle John and their sons William and Steven until her death. My close relationship with her survived until her death in Strathcarron Hospice.

At No 1 Glebe Street, a few yards away, was my father's family home. His mother had also died when the family was relatively young so my granda' Delaney, Auld Lukie, relied on his eldest daughter, my Aunt Janet, to support him in bringing up his eight sons and two other daughters. Both my mother and father's families lived near to each other and knew each other well, long before any relationships developed. Aunt Janet and

Uncle Wullie were qualified mental health nurses and worked in Larbert Hospital many years before me.

I have been told for my whole life that I was Wullie's double and that when I was a baby, he even said, "Michael is the only one who is like me." That statement perplexed me for decades, as he was absolutely right. I don't remember him, he died when I was a small child, but I have had complete strangers approach me to say how much like him I was, not so much in looks, but in personality and mannerisms. This strongly suggests to me therefore, that he was also gay although I have never found any clear evidence of this as it was illegal whilst he was alive. My mum was very close to my Uncle Wullie and he was much loved by all who knew him, this flamboyant, outrageous man who could entertain a room full of people with his antics.

I have clear recollection of feeling needy as a child and fearing abandonment by my mother. In 1964 when I was four, she went into hospital for an extended period due to complications in her pregnancy with my sister Eileen. I don't remember being told anything about where she was. I was sent to stay with my Aunt Frances and Uncle Robert and simply remember the feeling of desertion, abandonment and not knowing if she was ever coming back. It was the era of 'children should be seen and not heard' so information was not passed on to us. I was grief stricken and remember the joy when I returned home several weeks later when she came back from hospital with my new sister. It was following this that I became ever more insecure and attached to my mother; fearing that if she left the house to go anywhere, she may not return.

This resulted in me becoming very clingy, constantly demanding to be ever present on her travels. "Mum! Where are ye going? Where are ye going? Can I come? Can I come? Can I come?" Eventually I would wear my mum down and she would take me with her. Not only did I know that she wouldn't disappear so long as I was keeping an eye on her, I had her full attention on a one-to-one basis for as long as the activity lasted. This fear of abandonment varied in its intensity but was ever-present.

There was one incident when my father was managing the local branch of the British Legion and my mum used to work as a waitress in the lounge bar at night. On this particular night, both of them were quite drunk when they got back from work and my mum was arguing with my dad, accusing him of looking at other women. It became very heated due to the levels of alcohol and as I lay in bed crying, I could hear my dad lose his temper and hit my mum. It was the only time he ever hit her, but I will never forget the feeling of my world crashing down around me; the terror of what could happen and the fear of them splitting up. I had no control. I was a child, and I couldn't do anything. I was powerless to prevent the two people who I loved most from hurting each other. My brother John and I simply huddled together and cried. My older brothers pretended to be asleep, but I knew they were also crying silently.

By this time, I was around eight or nine years old, and my fear of abandonment advanced to a new level. I became very ill and stayed off school for a long time. Every time I was due to go back, I would relapse into this state of exhaustion and fatigue and become unable to function. I was pale and weak and underweight. Eventually I was sent to Stirling Royal Infirmary for tests and the provisional diagnosis was rheumatic fever.

During the summer holidays I regained my strength with lots of food and outdoor activities and I returned to St Patrick's the next term. In hindsight I can honestly say that the whole illness may well have been psychological in nature; triggered by my acute fear of abandonment. I believed that if I went to school, I may have come home one day and found I had no parents but if I stayed at home, I could prevent that from happening. The fragility of this family system intensified over these years. As both my parents worked at the British Legion, my eldest brother Luke became more and more powerful and added threat and intimidation to the many dynamics within our house. Having been the first born, he was placed in a sort of head of the household role, but unfortunately his performance was never monitored and at times he went totally out of control. He had a predilection for violence and was never happier than when he was drinking to excess and physically fighting any number of people, including family members. He absolutely ruled the roost and was seldom challenged about his methods. He damaged many people over his life and traumatised his siblings, particularly Alice, and he later repeated that same cycle of trauma on his own daughter Zoe. On one occasion when I was around fifteen, I had a group of friends from St Modan's visiting for a party. We were having a laugh and he arrived drunk and aggressive and wanted to put the TV on. "Luke, this is my night and you're not spoiling it because you want to watch TV!" I had said bravely. He lifted me off the floor by my throat and threw me backwards on to the couch in front of my friends and I stormed out of the living room feeling angry and ashamed. At that moment all the lights went out as the electricity needed ten pence in the metre. I was sitting in the dark, raging with anger, holding a carving knife in my hand. I could see him coming into the kitchen through the darkness so I stood up and tried to plunge the knife into him but, as the lights suddenly came back on, he quickly caught my arm and blocked the attack. I can still remember the look on his face. In that moment he realised that I would have stabbed him, and he was shocked.

From about the age of eight or nine I knew for sure that I was different from the rest of my family and from anyone else I knew who lived in my town. I loathed football and other contact sports, partly because I hated rough sports and getting dirty but also because I had worn glasses since I was two years old and they would be hit by the ball and broken regularly because I was so bad at football! I had a 'squint' in my left eye so apart from the constant sissy insults, I also had 'specky four eyes', 'the milky bar kid', and in the latter years 'joe 90' added to the entourage of abuse hurled at me! That doesn't include the extended periods when, following appointments at the Stirling Eye Clinic, I had to walk about with a large chunk of Elastoplast adhesive dressing covering my right lens to encourage my lazy eye to do more! How unhealthy for a self-conscious child to spend months looking like that. They never had to search out names for me, they were there for all to see. Thank goodness I was given a resilient and humorous personality as part of the deal!

In one of my many attempts to escape the pressure to comply with society's norms and due to the fear of what the future might hold for me, I decided that the catholic priesthood was for me. I would be away from all the people who called me names; I would be surrounded by priests who were gentle and behaved well and I would be able to say mass and benediction from the altar. I often wondered how many boys actually joined the priesthood for the same reasons as I almost did. Interesting piece of research I think!

My religious conversion and new, spiritual lifestyle, was also directly linked to the influence of Mrs Mc Peake, a gifted and dedicated teacher who was a devoted catholic and who worked tirelessly throughout my school years to have Blessed

John Ogilvie canonised a Saint. She was a powerful and influential woman who inspired many pupils to work hard and achieve better things for themselves. She wore her religion like a badge and, in many ways taught children to be themselves and to stand in their own truth. I adored being in her class and loved her teaching methods. She was charismatic, endlessly patient and inspired self-belief in all of her students, regardless of ability. When Mrs Mc Peake arrived for work in the morning and left to go home at night, she was surrounded by crowds of eager children clambering to carry her bag and to tell her all their news. She never made anyone feel unworthy and spent considerable time ensuring she had spoken to all of them.

As part of my new-found vocation I managed to beg, steal and borrow some religious memorabilia from around the family, a statue, some candlesticks, some holy pictures, a linen cloth and a long red rug. With my collection of 'holy artefacts,' I proceeded to make an altar on the high mantelpiece of the fireplace in my shared bedroom. When someone climbed over piles of dirty clothes, shoes, toys, two sets of bunk beds and a double bed there stood my altar resplendent in its second-hand glory. I spent long periods celebrating mass at my altar and serving communion to whoever was present in the living room, wearing a shirt and nylon raincoat back to front as my priest-outfit. "The body of Christ...Amen" could be heard around the room as people tried to watch television and chat.

On one particular evening, I remember being in bed next to my brother John who was asleep. I was lying staring at my altar and dreaming about the day when I would leave this place and become a holy priest, when my older brother Andrew came into the room to go to bed.

He got into his pyjamas and, before he got into his bunk,

knelt at my altar to say his evening prayers. In my state of 'perpetual grace', I sat up in bed and screamed, "Get away from my fucking altar!" at the top of my lungs. Unfortunately for me, my mother was walking past the bedroom door at the time and in her own inimitable way said, "How very religious! A priest? A bloody priest?" before dragging me from the bottom bunk and thumping the daylights out of me. Needless to say, I had to tone down my religious aspirations after that incident as my foul language had clearly brought my sincerity into question. Not surprisingly, the desire to escape remained intact and my religious leanings simply varied in their levels of commitment. Priest? Marist Brother? Monk? They were all real possibilities, and they all gave me a way of escaping what I could only imagine was going to be my living nightmare of a future. This desire intensified further as I approached twelve years of age and had to contemplate going to St Modan's High School seven miles away and starting the process all over again with several hundred new pupils who I was sure were also going to hate me.

My first few days in Broadway Lodge were very busy and often quite profound, even when simply chatting between groups, gaining insights into my own addictions through listening to others share their war-stories. The first assignment, as I touched on above, was to write my life-story and present it to the group who then give you feedback about themes and behaviours which emerge as you tell your story to them, allowing them to get to know you a bit better as well. It's a big piece of work to try to remember so many things and to get them down on paper in a few days and the thought of having to then read it out to my therapy group and counsellor was causing me some anxiety. I wrote things I had never owned before, about myself and about my family; about our dysfunction, violence in the home, the impact of religion, double standards and of sexual abuse from an unknown stranger which occurred when I was around seven years old at 'The Gala,' a trauma which I pushed down to a deep place and never told a living soul about. I could never understand it or find the words to describe what happened and how traumatised and confused it left me feeling about myself. Instead, I believed it must have been my fault and if I spoke out, I would be punished.

I remember sitting in my group room next to the reception area with eight or nine other patients in my group and my focal counsellor who I had read it to the day before. My counsellor introduced me and asked the group to listen carefully for themes such as self-pity or denial which I could then work on in treatment. The room fell silent and I began to read my 'shameful' story.

As my storytelling progressed, I noticed that the silence was being pierced by tearful gasps and as I looked up from my page for the first time, I could see that the majority of my group members, both male and female were crying. "What are you crying for?" I asked in a puzzled yet quite aggressive tone.

I received a unified response from all of them. "What you have said is very sad and very traumatic!"

I then became defensive and said loudly, "It wasn't traumatic because everyone in my neighbourhood was in the same boat, it was the norm!"

My counsellor signalled for the group to settle and quietly said to me, "Michael, because it was happening to everyone else doesn't make it right. What you describe is very painful for a child to comprehend and accept without there being long term damage.

"We are not saying your family were bad, we are saying maybe they did their best; but it fell short and is a factor in why you are here." At that point I remember thinking "Oh God, what is happening to me." I felt a tidal wave of emotion surge through my body with an intensity I had never experienced. As I was about to ask to leave the group, in a completely involuntary way, I exploded into uncontrollable tears, and feeling ashamed of my tears as well as my story, I tried to leave the room.

My peers blocked me. Not in an aggressive way, in a kind and compassionate way. In a way I had seldom experienced, putting arms around me, asking me to stay, assuring me that I would benefit if I had courage and did not allow shame to block my feelings. I was in shock, terrified, I didn't know what to do. My counsellor guided me and reassured me as I got back into my seat and at that moment he said, "Michael, just breathe, listen, and we will come back to your life story in a few minutes."

He then asked the group if they could offer me any support in my situation. One by one they shared painful experiences which they had only disclosed since coming into treatment, some similar to mine and some much worse. Every one of them ended by saying, "I felt just like you not so long ago but by facing the fear and the shame I am now much stronger and less ashamed." It was a very strange feeling; being seen and heard, maybe for the first time, and it was enough to stop me from running. I took a few long deep breaths and continued my story which finally ended forty minutes later.

"…and a few days ago I came to this place in the hope that I would find some answers and stop trying to kill myself."

As I looked back up from my paper I was deafened by the noise of applause and everyone was on their feet, crying through their smiles, but congratulating and affirming me for my courage and strength. For the first time in my life, I felt valued and heard, not judged and condemned. I sat for a few minutes with tears streaming down my face as every group member approached me, congratulated me and gave me the most generous hugs and pats on the back. Eventually, as with the closing of all groups in Broadway Lodge, we stood in a circle, held hands and said the serenity prayer, "God, grant me the serenity, to accept the things I cannot change, the courage to change the things I can, and the wisdom to know the difference." That simple prayer was soon to become my mantra in every difficult situation and often gave me breathing space to find a solution or to get out of a risky situation.

I remember going back into the lounge for a coffee and the atmosphere was electric as everyone had released their tears, and with them, painful feelings. This naturally developed into hysterical humour and within a short space of time the tears had been replaced by belly laughter like I had never experienced. In a situation like that, when a group of people have experienced the same horrific pain, the intensity of the connection between peers is at a level seldom experienced in normal life. To feel safe enough to let someone into your pain and to have that reciprocated by them openly sharing their pain with you is a true privilege which intensifies that connection as time moves forward. The love you feel for one another is strong and real and is the first example of experiencing feelings without blotting them out with chemicals.

Following my Life-Story there was a session called Peer-Evaluation where my group members completed an exercise highlighting the issues which they felt were serious and needed to be addressed by me in treatment. There were several areas identified; including caretaking and minimising, but the main observation from everyone was anger. I was shocked that people thought I was angry and I felt upset that it wasn't just one or two but all of them. "I'm not angry." I protested as each of them read out their findings and I found myself become overwhelmed that the strongest impression I gave off was anger. At the end of the group I stayed behind and asked my counsellor what I should do.

"Listen to what your peers are telling you," he said.

"But I'm not angry," I replied, as calmly as I could.

He sighed slightly then took a breath and said, "I would like you to go away and write down a list of a hundred resentments that you carry and we will process them together in our session later."

"I don't have a hundred resentments!" I protested, but he looked at me and said, "Just do it, Mike."

I grabbed a cup of coffee and headed to a quiet room with my ring binder and a pen and sat down to start this impossible assignment. 'How could I possibly carry so many resentments? He must have made a mistake. I'm a nice person, a nurse for God's sake!' I thought to myself. I opened the page and began to write and was shocked at how quickly my list grew, and before I knew it, I had written the hundredth line. It took me seven minutes to list a hundred resentments which I wasn't even consciously aware of holding on to. I was totally shocked, resentments are anger held against people, places or things outside of self. Maybe my peers were right, maybe I was overflowing with anger, and because of this resented so many people. I had also read somewhere that suicide was the ultimate act of anger against oneself, I could feel my defences beginning to crumble.

After lunch I went for my one-to-one session with Stefan, my counsellor. He asked me to read out my list and then we would talk about it afterwards, so I began the rundown of my chart. My top ten I remember, included Margaret Thatcher, Paul Daniels and Debbie McGhee. After a five-minute discussion about why I held so much anger towards Mrs Thatcher, he said, "Why Paul Daniels?" And I could feel the anger rising again.

"Because he's an arrogant, unfunny, talentless little shit!" I said through gritted teeth.

"And Debbie McGhee?" he asked.

"Because she married that little fucker!" I immediately snapped.

Eventually Stefan summarised the session and said, "Can you see how much anger you carry in order to hold such resentment against other people, most of whom have no bearing whatsoever on your life, and who are oblivious to the hatred you feel for them. Whilst you are being poisoned with this toxic anger, they are getting on with their lives unaware of your existence." In that moment, the light bulb switched-on. I clearly saw the madness of my thought processes and the damage I was doing to myself, by indulging in such negative thought patterns. I smiled at Stefan, but at the same time, tears fell from my eyes as I understood my own part in making myself feel so angry and resentful. Once again, I could see that my behaviour was ultimately based in self-loathing and the person I always hurt most was myself.

'Whether you think you can or think you can't, you're right.'
—Henry Ford

Reflection on moving to St Modan's High

I remember being terrified at the thought of leaving St Pat's and moving to the High School in Stirling. St Modan's was a very good High School and had a wide catchment area covering all of the Stirling area including Raploch, Cowie, Fallin and Cambusbarron, stretching all the way over to some areas of Falkirk and Kilsyth. There were fleets of buses every day bringing pupils from all over the area to St Ninians and the loud singing of Celtic songs could often be heard before the buses arrived. Some areas had a bad reputation due to poverty and deprivation such as Denny, Raploch and Cowie and the school could at times, understandably, be tribal. We stuck together when things emerged that could threaten us, and we protected our own.

I still felt very different from my peers, but I had spent seven years with my class at St Pat's and generally felt safe and secure in my friendships and my position within the hierarchy. I had heard horrific stories about the bullying at St Modan's and of first year pupils being 'ducked,' having their head put down the toilet and flushed. Three of my older siblings had all attended and had various shocking anecdotes to recall when the subject of school came up, including my brother Luke being suspended for hanging a teacher out of a fourth-floor window by his feet following an altercation about money. One of the benefits of these events for me was the fact that my brothers had earned a bit of a reputation so, unbeknownst to me, several of the wilder pupils were a bit reticent to pick on me for fear of retribution.

Before finally accepting my fate and agreeing to go to St Modan's I had a final Ace up my sleeve. Having toyed with the idea of a religious calling in my younger days and having spoken to visiting priests, I had made the decision that the priesthood felt too restrictive for me and the parish life, although very fulfilling, was repetitive and difficult work. How could I become a priest when I became thoroughly bored in every church service within a few minutes? I found the slow drone of the priest's voice combined with the dated and punishing language to be like a sedative and, within minutes I would be nodding off or giggling with whoever I was sitting with. This often ended with slaps from complete strangers if I wasn't with my um, who would happily provide those slaps!

The next best thing to the priesthood which would also enable me to avoid going to St Modan's was to become a Marist Brother! They had a facility in the south of Scotland which was like a boarding school and their reputation was very high regarding the standard of education. At the end of your time, you became a religious brother, which seemed to be less restrictive than the priesthood, but still provided a certain status and respect. Several people from my hometown had done the same thing and I would occasionally see them wearing a black Barathea blazer with a small motive on the breast pocket, rather like a school blazer. Although I liked the idea of a priest's collar, I was willing to make sacrifices in order to avoid St Modan's. I got the information pack and application and brought them home one day to discuss with my parents.

My plan was set, and I chose my time, directly after our dinner when they were full-up and settling down in front of the television, after the news but not during anything interesting on Nationwide or Reporting Scotland with Mary Marquis. As always, our living room was packed with bodies on all of the chairs and all over the floor so there was never going to be a private moment to unveil my masterplan. I took a breath, handed over the pile of paperwork and said, "Can you sign this so that I can become a Marist Brother?" There was a very momentary silence, before what felt like everyone in the room beginning to laugh hysterically.

"You! A Marist Brother, what a joke!" My brother Luke bellowed as he choked on his tea. "You must be kidding!" came another response. "You're gaun tae Hell, how can ye be a Marist Brother!" yet another person said.

My usual well-versed response of, "Shut it!" came screaming out as I tried to salvage my plan from eternal damnation. "I don't want to be like you and work in a foundry, I want to be a Marist Brother!"

My dad had managed to retain a fairly straight face although I could see the corners of his mouth fighting the urge to smile. "Where the hell has this come from?" he said as he placed a Capstan in his mouth and looked for his Ronson lighter to finish the ritual. "You would need to sleep in a big dormitory with lots of strangers and you wouldn't be able to come home except in the holidays," he said, expecting that statement to change my mind whereas it made the whole concept more appealing to me!

"I know dad, but I would be OK and I would make new friends there and be happy," I pleaded desperately. I saw my dad's motivation to continue coaxing me wane somewhat as This is Your Life was beginning and he always liked the surprise, unless it was someone like Lulu or Petula Clarke whom he loathed. He averted his gaze from me and looked at my mum to make the final decision.

She looked at me with disconnected eyes and said, "Yer no gaun tae nae Marist Brothers. It coasts too much money and I need ye here! Yer gaun tae St Modan's like everybody else!" she roared as she threw the pile of papers back at me. "Yer a Delaney, no a Gruba!" She was referring to a neighbouring family who had a couple of sons become Marist Brothers, and that was her final nail in the coffin.

As the room echoed with shaming laughter and sarcastic retorts, I gathered up my papers and as I began to exit the room I turned in shame and shouted, "I fuckin' hate you lot!" before seeing the shock on my mum's face and running for my life up the hallway, out of the front door and away from her outstretched arms.

When everything had settled and I felt safe enough to come back into the house I sat in my chaotic room where five of us slept in a variety of beds, with clothes, toys and rubbish all over the floor, and thought to myself as I looked around the carnage, "How can a dormitory be worse than this? At least it would be tidy!" I felt the fat tears begin to trickle down my cheeks and threw myself dramatically onto a bed and began to sob. My dream was over, my plan foiled and I now had no choice but to go to St Modan's. I felt the anxiety enter my body as I began to face the reality of my future.

As my final term at St Patrick's ended, I felt very sad and unsure of the future. My friend Michael Kelly (not the same Michael Kelly who is referred to later in my story), who had lost his dad suddenly in a hit and run accident was moving back to Perth with his mum Kareen and his siblings. They invited me to stay for a holiday so for the first time in my life, at age twelve, I packed a bag and got on a bus for what seemed like a long journey, all the way from Denny to Perth, for two weeks. I had never travelled alone or stayed out of the house for more than an occasional night at a relative's house and here I was spending two whole weeks in a faraway city. I was so excited to be away from my family and able to have fun. The Kellys had moved into a brand-new house in an estate and were starting from scratch after the terrible trauma they had gone through. In hindsight I can see that Kareen was still very much in shock and trying to come to terms with her devastating loss. She and her husband Michael were very much in love when he was taken, and I remember seeing her sitting crying on several occasions during my stay. I had a fantastic two weeks away and am convinced that it was then that I got my itchy feet and began to believe that there were better and more exciting opportunities outside of Denny.

On my return home all I could think about was the terror of starting high school. The threats had already started from older boys. "Just you wait. You're getting ducked" could be heard from passing groups of boys. "There's no escape, you're getting drowned!" I would lie in bed at night and try to think of ways to avoid the inevitable, but I could not top my Marist Brother plan, and if I suggested anything which remotely suggested that I wasn't going my mum would simply stare at me and say, "Aye, yer gaun!"

The day arrived and I was dressed in my almost new uniform, a new shirt and tie, but the black flannels and blazer had belonged to my cousin Pat McNally. Luckily Pat really looked after his clothes, so I was actually quite happy to wear his hand-me-downs. I crossed Glebe Street to meet Joe Smith for the bus, and we met Brian McPeake and Pat McCafferty en-route to the Stirling bus stop. We were all a bit nervous, but it was also quite an exciting experience.

As we arrived at what seemed to be an enormous school, compared to St Pat's, with older two storey buildings and four storey modern blocks, we had to find out where we were supposed to be, so we headed to an area in the refectory where everyone's name, form, class and classroom were listed. We were all separated at that point and put in different form-classes, I could feel the panic set in as we wandered the maze of corridors trying to find our form room. I finally found my Class, One-A, in the French Corridor, and thankfully I knew some of my former classmates who were also in my new class. As I walked around the grounds on my first few days, I could see lots of smaller boys drenched in water where they had already been ducked in the toilets. I resolved to piss myself rather than go anywhere near a toilet! As it transpired, my hand-me-down blazer seemed to save me, as people thought I was in second year and I was never ducked!

After settling-in, for the most part I loved St Modan's. I made strong friendships with people from all over the area, however Pat, Brian and Joe remained my core friendships well into adolescence. One or two others also joined us in that clique, namely Paul Morgan from Raploch and Vincent Connolly from Dunblane. They regularly came through to Denny and stayed over at weekends and would join us at the YM for a few drinks and a dance. Sadly, I attended Vincent's funeral in Stirling in 2020 after hearing he had passed from Huntington's Disease.

Paul Morgan became a particularly strong friend of mine because we were in the same form-class and spent a lot of time together, and I could make him laugh without any effort. How I loved getting him into trouble by making him laugh in class. He could not laugh quietly and the teacher always caught him! He lived in Ochil Crescent, Raploch, and like me, had several brothers and sisters, the most infamous one being Frankie Morgan who was a skinhead and wore turned-up jeans just below the knee, and cherry red Doc Martins that you could see your face in. He was quite an aggressive individual and, for a time, ruled the school and was 'respected' by all of the pupils. I remember one day being in their house in Raploch. We were in Paul's bedroom which was painted completely black, listening to a New

York Dolls album when Frankie kicked the door in and said, "Run, fuckers!" as he loaded an air rifle with pellets. I looked at Paul and we both screamed and ran as fast as we could out of the house, but he was right on our tail, and as we ran towards Stirling Bridge in hysterical laughter I could hear pellet after pellet whizz past my head. Eventually he stopped and we fell into a heap of laughter on the ground.

Paul was also a bit different in terms of his personality within his family. Like me, he had interests other than football and didn't connect much with his brothers, so we became very close. He was quite sensitive and could be emotional at times, but he was a good person and really cared about people. By the time we were in our fourth year and thinking about careers etc., I was planning on Hotel Management and had chosen my subjects for coming back to do a fifth and sixth year with the possibility of university (my mum had other ideas for my employment but that's another story!). Paul was also doing further study and then, suddenly there was what was called 'A Mission' at St Modan's. The fourth years were invaded by priests, monks, religious brothers and nuns for a whole week, trying to recruit for the Church. By this time, I had long accepted that my religious leanings were absolutely nothing to do with God but were just an avoidance technique I had devised to get me out of high school! However, I saw a look on Paul's face that I had never seen before. He was visibly excited by what was discussed and he spent long hours talking to different priests and brothers. It was a very lovely time and we spent long periods in the main hall singing folk hymns with live musicians and choirs and clapping which was unheard of in 1976. I still remember the energy when they belted out, "Walk with me Oh my Lord, through the darkest nights and brightest days…" It was like a giant party and everyone seemed so happy and connected. Then the mission was over and my mindset returned to matters at hand; who was going to the YM this week?

Little did I know that Paul did not switch off from the mission. It had entered his being in a way that no-one saw until later in the year when my career plans had changed and myself, Pat and Brian were all working in Larbert Hospital as nursing assistants. We met a nurse whilst playing truant before the summer holidays and she asked if we would like to volunteer. We did and loved it so much we never went back to school! We still saw Paul occasionally on weekends, he had a part time job somewhere, then, without warning, following a wild drunken party at his Auntie Julia's house in Stirling he disappeared and joined the priesthood. He stayed in touch for a short time, by letter and made the odd trip to The McCafferty's house in Glebe Street, but then we heard he had been called to Rome to work in the Vatican. I never heard from him again and always wondered how he was or what he was up to. Many years later I heard that he had left the priesthood and was a teacher somewhere in Edinburgh, but by then I was in England and was never able to re-connect. I still think of him often and hope that wherever he is and whatever he is doing, he is happy.

'Do what you can with all you have, wherever you are.'
—Theodore Roosevelt

Step One

I remember sitting in Broadway Lodge one evening, writing step one; examples of people I had hurt through my addiction and my old friend Philomena McCoy came to my mind. We met in 1987 when I started working as a CPN and I was based in a

Portakabin in the grounds of Leytonstone House in East London.

Phil was a charge nurse in the main hospital and had worked there for a short time after moving from Ireland to live with her partner a few years previously. Unfortunately, the relationship did not work out, so she threw herself into her job and social life. We met one day as she passed by my office and my colleague Ben called her in to meet me.

"This is Mike Delaney who has recently joined the team," he said as he gestured towards me. "And this is Phil McCoy," he said as he put his arm around her shoulders. She was shorter than Ben and had long red hair and freckles and was very open and friendly.

"Hi, Mike, lovely to meet you," she said with a broad smile. "Where do you live? Do you fancy coming for a drink with the crowd in The North Star?"

"That would be lovely," I said, "but not tonight as I have another engagement."

"Ok well, let me know when it suits you and I can introduce you to everyone in the pub," she said before heading back out to her meeting.

I was lying; I did not have another engagement as such, but my partner Peter was suffering from depression and was not in a good place, so I wanted to get back and make sure he was ok. I had recently called his bluff when he was suicidal and suggested we do it together as I didn't want to deal with the aftermath of his death. I had no intention but was trying to show him the enormity of his actions on those left behind. It had served to stall him but I was still concerned.

Although we didn't know each other well Philomena went out of her way to make sure I met 'The Gang' which included Ian and Steve, Sandra, Anne and a number of day staff and nurses whom she knew. The reason Phil had come into my head writing step one was because I didn't always treat her well and she often became the focus of my anger when I felt overwhelmed as she had a strong personality and would often unintentionally trigger my anger. When this happened, I would unleash a barrage of insults against her, often in front of others in order to maximise the impact of her shame. I particularly remembered an incident in a pub called Lincolns where a crowd of us were sitting drinking one evening and for some reason she chose that moment to suggest that I was a bit 'messed-up' and should maybe think about seeing a counsellor.

In hindsight I knew that it was coming from a place of love and concern, but in that moment it felt like all of my barriers had been removed and I was naked and vulnerable. I proceeded to launch into a tirade about her physical appearance, her weight, her lack of a relationship, every single weakness I could find was named and shamed, making the whole group uncomfortable, which subsequently led to outbursts of awkward laughter. I can still see Phil's face looking at mine's with an expression which simply said, "Why are you doing this to me?" before her lower lip began to tremble and tears began to pour down her cheeks.

Despite her expression I was unable to contain my anger and continued to berate her until she had finally had enough and left.

That night, sitting in Broadway Lodge, was the first time I had consciously thought about the events of that evening and how cruel and unrelenting I had been. I felt a deep shame come over my body and envelop me as I began to sob for the deep hurt which I had caused someone who, despite everything, had only ever loved and cared for me.

A year or two later I happened to be in East London visiting my sister when I decided it was time to 'work on my programme' and to make amends with Phil. We had lost touch in 1995 after Michael Kelly's death but I knew she had a flat in Leyton so decided to surprise her. Nervously I looked at the intercom button before taking a deep breath and pressing. "Hello." The familiar voice came through the little speaker.

"Well hello, Sister McCoy," I replied.

"Oh my God! Michael!" She didn't unlock the door, she came running down the stairs, burst through the main door and threw her arms around me continually saying, "Oh Jesus! Oh my God! Where have you been?" It was a lovely welcome and, after what I have just described, completely undeserved, but I went with it and climbed the stairs to her flat to begin the story of where I had been.

She was shocked but delighted to hear that I had been to rehab and had been clean for around eighteen months or so. We talked, drank tea, talked more, laughed and drank more tea until I said, "Phil, one of the reasons I'm here is that, in working on my recovery programme I am making amends with anyone who I've hurt and there is an incident that I feel really bad about..." As I looked into her eyes, I could see the recognition of the evening which I was about to address and she began to spontaneously cry. I had hurt her so badly that I didn't even have to jog her memory, it was there just below the surface.

"Can you remember..." I said before being interrupted by her trying to speak through her tears.

"You don't have to apologise, Mike... It doesn't matter... I understand..." she said, in the hope that I would shut up, but I wouldn't.

"Phil, I want to do this for you, but also for me," I said as I held her hand and began to cry myself. "That night in Lincolns is one of the most horrific things I have done to anyone and I want you to know how deeply sorry and ashamed I am of my behaviour that night and of the pain I caused you through my behaviour," I slowly managed to say, through snot and tears. She held onto my hands tightly and sobbed loudly, saying, "It's OK Mike; I forgive you, don't worry, it's OK" before both of us simply held each other and cried together, until we both settled and regained our composure.

A very emotional but beautiful healing moment, almost ten years after the event had taken place. I have worked my programme many times over the years, in making amends with people when an opportunity arises and it is usually a similarly powerful moment, most people do not ever get that apology or explanation. There is such power in apologising and in forgiveness

Many years later I was home in Denny for a concert which was being held in the Crypt where different musicians and bands from the area were playing. It was so exciting to go into a packed Crypt and see so many familiar faces I hadn't seen for so long. I think it was the last time I saw Auntie Peggy who was there with Elizabeth. The main music between acts was being provided by John Murphy whom I was surprised to see was being supported by my old friend Louise on keyboards.

I looked at the stage and smiled at Louise whom I hadn't seen for many years and who I remembered having been vile towards on the last occasion I had seen her, probably twenty years before. I couldn't remember the actual content of the event but I remembered saying some horrible things to her. I knew that I had to apologise if an opportunity arose that evening. As it happened, between the acts she sat down with the Grant sisters, so I was able to sit with them all and have a blether. I said to Louise, "Can we have a few words before you go back on stage?" I could see the same expression on her face as was on Phil's a couple of years before.

We moved away to a couple of empty seats in a booth and I said, "Louise, I need to apologise for something…" That was all I managed to say before she stopped me firmly and said, "Michael, we've all done things we regret and I've also hurt you in the past so why don't we just draw a line under it and move forward. I've got to go back on that stage and smile in a minute and I can't if there's mascara all over ma face wae greetin'!" she said with a wry smile. I simply nodded in acceptance of her compromise and we had a cuddle. Thankfully we have remained friends and I saw her as recently as last year for lunch where we laughed for hours.

These painful snapshots were a regular part of exploring past events and building a foundation of stone which could deter the desire to return to alcohol or drugs. I don't sit and think about painful memories all day as that would undoubtedly make me want to drink or use, however, in the scope of writing step one I remember as much as possible in the hope of convincing myself that there is no fun left in the addictive process – only pain and heartache. It is a very effective deterrent against the temptation to return to old behaviours and has kept me sober since 1996.

There is also a hugely positive energy in a group of people who are having the same painful realisations and the mutual support which develops is hugely beneficial and healing for all concerned. As we re-connect with others in a new and powerful way we realise that superficiality is actually not fully connecting, but honesty and authenticity creates strong and lasting bonds.

Pubs

When examining my past, I had to look at the choices I made and the situations I found myself in. Since turning eighteen and right through my twenties, I worked in pubs at night and over the weekends. I enjoyed the social aspect and the hard work which was involved, but I also loved the fact that I was immersed in alcohol culture and could drink, as I worked, for free.

In my hometown Denny this habit began in the newly opened Lion and Dragon which was a large retail premises in the Church Walk Development opposite the post office on Duke Street. It comprised of a large function suite, a smaller lounge bar and a large Chinese restaurant initially – hence the name and the symbolism of the Scottish Lion and Chinese Dragon. The Chinese partner in the business pulled out after a time and it was taken over as a separate entity by an Asian businessman who opened Omar Khayyam, an Indian restaurant which still operates today in another part of the town centre. For the first few weeks I worked in the function suite only, so was lucky to see some great cabaret acts such as Christian, while I was working behind the bar. It started off well, with good sized crowds and waitress service only at tables, but the residential accommodations upstairs were tortured by the noise levels as there was no soundproofing to speak of. Eventually the council got involved because of the number of complaints and installed a 'Trip-Switch' which cut off all electricity to the stage equipment immediately if the sound passed a certain decibel level. This was not a good intervention, most of the acts were being cut-off mid performance, particularly singers who built their voices for a big finish. Both performers and audiences got fed up and gradually the functions died-off, as the owners had to sell a minimum number of tickets to pay for the better-known acts. Eventually the function suite was converted to a snooker hall for a time, before finally ending its life as Sylvester's Nightclub which, I understand, had invested in soundproofing!

Before the cabaret nights ended at The Dragon, I was lured away by an offer of work at the Don-R-Inn which had opened a disco in a newly built extension and had a serving licence that lasted until one a.m. on Friday and Saturday nights. The place was packed soon after opening its doors at seven-thirty p.m. There were usually four bouncers on duty, two at main door and two at the lounge door, me and two other bar-staff usually Maria Donoghue and Jemima Thompson whose sister Margaret worked behind the disco bar. My sister Alice also came in when we needed her at different points. It was extremely hard work, without breaks, but we had such a laugh as we worked and, at intervals, we would mix cocktails for ourselves from the many drinks we were bought by the punters. The music was provided by a young Frank McCafferty who shared the decks, with Ally McKillop, and the dance floor was seldom empty. However, The Donner was one of those places you had to observe closely because later in the evening as the young males tried to impress the young females very often a switch would be tripped and all hell would break loose. Because of the close-knit relationships in a small town, the initial disagreements between two people would spread like wildfire as punches were thrown and countless other people jumped-in to defend their friends or family members. This often also included women who would get torn-in with all the men.

I used to make a joke when we opened the doors that the first few women who would come up to the bar and say, "Two Carlsberg Specials please, Michael", would by eleven p.m., be screaming "Get me a fuckin' Carlsberg! I've been staunin' here for fuckin' hours ya bunch of lazy bastards!" That particular drink had the capacity to transform personality types from the shy wallflower, to Boadicea on her chariot! When the fighting started it could be vicious, so even if it was nowhere near the bar, our immediate protocol was to pull the shutters down and lock the bar off. We then waited to see if it was going to be a small scuffle or if it was going to be a spreader, like in a cowboy saloon! Sometimes the bouncers would quickly isolate it and remove the offenders in which case we were allowed to reopen, but more often than not it became a free-for-all and we began washing up the glasses as we knew it was going to be an early night. As I was also a nurse, that being my day-job, I sometimes had to go out into the battlefield to administer first aid as pint glasses would often be used as weapons and could wound seriously and deeply. On several occasions I had to drag blood-soaked victims into the bar area and apply pressure to deep gashes whilst waiting for ambulances.

Despite all of that, I loved my time at the Don-R-Inn as they had a great staff team who made a laugh out of everything. I remember the manager Ben, who was an older guy and enjoyed a drink, approached me one evening and told me how tired he was. "Is there any chance you could manage this place for a week so that I can have a break?"

I told him I would have to check my own job and see if I was due holidays, but that if I could, I would. I managed to get a week off and the following week I was opening the bar at eleven a.m.

on a Monday. The bar was quite small with seating built into the windows, and a pool-table in the centre which was the focal point for most people. Denny at that time was still fairly small so everyone knew each other. The bar was busy and different people drifted in and out during the day. The licensing laws at that time meant it closed at three p.m. and reopened at five p.m. until eleven p.m. One of the things I remember most clearly is the sound of laughter when all the characters were bantering with each other. Rapid fire humour which was relentless and hysterical, one of the punters was always in the firing line, having to grin and bear it when something they had done was being lampooned. Eventually the torture would end and the victim would be bought a drink for putting up with all the ribbing, however, if you couldn't hack it there was no let-up and the humiliation continued, often ending with a "Fuck the lot of ye!" as the door slammed behind them.

Even young kids could skilfully make their feelings known. A few years earlier on Hogmanay, we were all sitting in the Railway Hotel pool room, which back then was in the small lounge to the left as you walked through the main door. It was early evening, around six p.m. and the atmosphere was merry as everyone made their plans for 'The Bells' and where they might be going. The Juke box was playing and there was a line of coins on the pool table showing the queue for a game. The door opened and a small boy of maybe nine years old came in with a heavy satchel full of evening papers. He slowly made his was around everyone in the room saying, "You want a paper?" and was told, "No thanks, pal" by everyone. As he opened the door to leave, without selling a single paper, he turned to the crowd and said loudly, "And a happy new year to the fuckin' lot of ye!" The place went into uproar with laughter and his cheek paid-off because everyone then bought papers and he left a happy boy!

After a few years in the Don-R-Inn I was offered bar work in The Railway Hotel which had just been bought and fully refurbished. I was mainly in the upstairs lounge as it was a very busy bar, hosting live music, DJs and quiz nights. It was a very small corner bar so a bit of a squeeze to work in, but we had some great laughs. Anne the owner, her friend Debbie, Carole, Grant, Aileen McMullan and I worked together at different times, laughing our heads off as we went. The Railway Hotel was the place to be at that time and was always very busy both upstairs and down. John Grant ran a football sweep and could always be heard shouting, "You owe me ten pound!" as someone tried to skulk away, which was often me! It felt like everyone in the town drank in the Railway at that time, it was a meeting place for a few drinks before going out to other places such as Le Clique in Stirling or The Maniqui in Falkirk. The next day in the bar was always the post-mortem of the previous night with a pub full of hangovers and funny stories. The patter was always first class with characters such as John Grant, wee Frankie Kelly, Hammy and Henry McGrorie sitting at the bar throwing one-liners across the room. Many times after I moved to England, I would make my way home for a few days break and would go into The Railway Hotel before I even went home, much to the disappointment of my mum, and I would trip to the family house only when the pubs shut! Before I left Denny The Railway Hotel was taken over by footballer Dom Sullivan who is still running it today although it is a much quieter affair these days. The whole pub-culture is much less popular than it used to be and there is also a lot less disposable income to throw around.

The Wee Band

Don't make friends who are comfortable to be with.
Make friends who will force you to lever yourself up.
—Thomas J. Watson

At that time, I was working days in Larbert and nights in pubs; I
was a member of a 'wee band', as the locals called it, and we
played in local places like the Lion and Dragon and The Railway
Hotel. In fact, John Twynholm, who owned The Dragon, helped
us to buy equipment, purchasing it for us then we played so many
gigs to pay for it which was a very kind gesture as there wasn't a
great deal of money kicking around in the late '70s and early
'80s. Our band started with Pat, Brian, Joe Smith and me messing
around with guitars in each other's houses, but eventually we
started to take it a bit more seriously and began to practice several
nights a week. Joe left and my brother John came in with a real
enthusiasm for lead and rhythm guitar; I played bass and
keyboard, Pat was rhythm guitar and Brian was drums. We got a
lot of support from Mick McNally and Robert McMullan who
had a popular band called Jade which later became Makaris Park,
and ultimately they became very successful as The Rocks.
Sometimes we would get The Church Crypt or The Lesser Hall
for practice so they would lend us all of their equipment
including Mick's Rickenbacker Bass which I loved to play as I
only had a cheap copy of a Fender Bass.

We had such fun playing in the band, covering a range of

music styles from The Eagles through to Lindisfarne, not always in a good way I might add! I will never forget the time we were booked to play a function at St Anne's Catholic Guild in the Lesser Hall. It was one of our early gigs and we set up our equipment and practiced in the afternoon. We sounded OK and planned our running order which was to begin with, Meet Me on the Corner, an old Lindisfarne number.

We looked at the audience of middle-aged to older Catholic women sitting at their tables and started the introduction. Brian sang lead on that song and came in on cue with the line 'Hey Mister Dream-Seller—' Unfortunately, it was before we had monitors and he was slightly flat. My brother John stopped playing and, forgetting we had a devout Catholic audience and were no longer practicing, shouted into the microphone, "Aw Brian, fur fuck's sake, ya tit!" There was an electric silence which fell over the hall as we stared at the women wondering if they had heard what had just been screamed through the amplifier. They sat in silence staring so we just said, "Sorry!" and restarted the song. They said that they enjoyed the evening but, unsurprisingly we were never invited back.

I used to disappear a lot and not practice. I had a very good ear for music and could pick it up quickly, but I was working two jobs and resented spending the little free time I had sitting at home practicing. I enjoyed the stage part as I could drink during the night but the sober evenings practicing at home were not my scene. I can see how frustrating that was for the other members, particularly John who was committed and enthusiastic but when I had the choice of the pub or practicing, guess what won. I would often come off the bus from Larbert and go into the record shop across from The Chapel where my friend Roseina Kelly worked, and when she closed-up we would head up to The Dragon and start drinking. On several occasions the bar door would be banged open and my fellow band members would be standing there with an exasperated look on their faces. "Aw fuckin' gimme a break!" I would yell and they would simply shake their heads and walk away except John who would be furious at my lack of commitment. "Yer a fuckin' waster, Michael! If this band splits up it's because of you!" he would shout.

At one point Alice and Roseina joined the band, and did guest spots singing solos and duets which was great and made us a little bit different at that time, but as far as I was concerned the writing was on the wall; I was starting to come to terms with moving away.

It's astounding when I look back, how young I was when alcohol became an important part of my survival. I felt so disconnected from most people, most of the time as I didn't feel able to be myself, and even a little alcohol or a spliff took the edge off my shame and self-loathing. Once I had had a lot of alcohol my mood was hugely altered and I didn't give a shit, although I still maintained my darkest secrets no matter how plastered I became.

'Stay strong. Even when it feels like everything's falling apart.'
—Anonymous

Step One Continued

Another night I was sitting in the lounge at Broadway, having a break from writing as it felt like I hadn't stopped in days, when I started chatting to Paul, who was a counsellor who had relapsed after being sober for some time. Although devastated by his return to old ways he was wise and had walked the walk for a good number of years. He started to share about the effect his drinking had on his wife and children, especially after being sober for a long period. This got me thinking in a new way about Susan and Clare, so I excused myself and went to the privacy of the committee room to begin writing.

I first met Susan at the Denny YMCA when we were about fifteen years old. She was from Falkirk so didn't attend my school, but I was seeing a girl called Caroline who lived in Falkirk so she had brought Susan, who began to see Pat McCafferty, and a girl called Hazel Graham who began to see Joe Smith. I remember the laughter, we often drunk alcohol before the disco and were a bit more confident than usual – particularly around Christmas when everyone was snogging under the mistletoe during the moon-dance section of the evening. This was after David Bowie, Marc Bolan and The Footsie had been blasted out. In amongst fights being broken up, there were teenagers falling in love and getting their lips 'red-raw wae the winchin'!' The YMCA was a rite of passage in Denny and was the highlight of an otherwise very dull existence.

The Catholic Church occasionally had a disco in the Lesser Hall or Boys Club Hall (I even remember a Record Hop before discos, hosted by the St Annes Guild) but they were often policed by the priest or pass-keepers from the Chapel so there was little fun to be had. I remember one dance in the boys-club hall which was interrupted by a very drunk Priest, Father Docherty, who eventually formed a circle and danced In and out those dusty bluebells to Devil-Gate Drive by Suzie Quatro! He must have been an alcoholic and was removed immediately after that night following his 'unprofessional behaviour'.

Anyway, as we approached sixteen years old, the YMCA lost its attraction, and as we began to shave, entry to pubs became the new developmental goal. Pat McCafferty reached that goal first as he had dark hair and his moustache showed. I was always blonde so my facial hair did not show, and I found it most difficult to be served. Indeed, on one of my travels to the US, aged 29, I was asked for proof of ID in a bar and was delighted!

I remember Joe Smith seeing Hazel for a while before he met Kate whom he is still happily married to, but Susan and the other Falkirk girls were reabsorbed back into the Falkirk scene and we lost touch for a while. Fast forward to 1978 and, after two years as a nursing assistant in a children's ward in Larbert, I was accepted to start my training as a registered nurse.

My first day was in the huts at Bellsdyke Hospital with John Baxter as the head of nurse training and Margaret Hannah who had been my ward sister in Lewis as a clinical teacher. I arrived nervously and met my class of fellow students. Some of them I knew from working in the juvenile hospital; so I wasn't so anxious, and then in walked Susan Woods who, unbeknown to me, was working as a nursing assistant in the adult hospital. We were so pleased to see each other and caught up on everything that had happened since we last met. Our friendship was re-ignited and for the next couple of years we were always together, socialising, studying, partying in large groups and arranging nights-out for the class. We were very close but never intimate. We both went out with other people and stayed good friends. I wish I had felt more able to tell people the truth about my sexuality, but things were different in Scotland in 1978 and I felt so ashamed of my sexuality that I never told a soul until several years later.

There were no mobile phones back then and not that many people had home phones, so communication could be difficult if you didn't see each other for a while. Our training consisted of educational blocks where we were together for eight weeks followed by several months of placements in a variety of settings, we could go for months without seeing each other unless there was a specific reason for us all to meet. By 1980 Susan had moved out of her family home in Falkirk and was renting a room from Lis, another class member. Lis and her husband Duncan lived across from the hospital, close to the Torwoodlea pub which was the main watering hole for the hospital. It had recently been fully refurbished and had added squash courts which were visible from the very posh cocktail bar. We spent many nights with groups of people unwinding and laughing our heads off in that place, most of the customers being colleagues, creating a safe space for ourselves.

It was after one of these nights when I had arranged to stay at Susan's place to study for our finals that our relationship changed. We had both had quite a bit to drink and were deciding to get some sleep, when we began to kiss. The kissing became more passionate, and we climbed into bed and began to make love. It was a powerful moment which soon impacted both of us, particularly Susan.

I remember not seeing her for a little while after that evening, which was not unusual, but then I was approached by a fellow student in the hospital grounds one day and she said, "You need to phone Susan. She's pregnant." I was shocked and felt dizzy with the news. 'How could this be?' I thought to myself. I didn't know what to do. It was 1980 and having children out of wedlock still had a stigma attached to it. 'Who will I talk to? How will I sort this out?' As always I closed my eyes and hoped it would go away without me having to deal with it, but I knew deep down that it wouldn't.

I remember feeling shell-shocked, and as I walked around the hospital, which was then a hot-bed of gossip, I wondered who already knew and who was judging me. I shared my news with Brian and Pat and Frank who looked more shocked than me and when I asked them what I should do they remained as blank as me. By this time I was living with my sister Alice in Overton Crescent, so I decided to call Susan at home that evening and see what was going on.

I sat in Alice's room, dialled the number and asked to speak to Susan. She came to the phone and said, "Hello?"

"Hi, it's Michael,' I said, "I heard you were pregnant."

After a small pause which suggested someone was nearby in her house she said, "Yeah, I am."

Completely unthinkingly I said, "Is it mine?" in that clumsy moment not realising the insult in the suggestion that she had been with other people. My memory following that call is pretty vague but I remember a defensive battle of words which ended in Susan hanging up the phone on me. I sat, in shock, shaking and frightened, tears flowing, wondering what the hell was going to happen. I felt more frightened of my family finding out than anything else. I composed myself and just hoped we could find a way through this dilemma. However time passed without any contact and my drinking began to escalate to ridiculous levels. I heard that Susan had the baby and I didn't know what to do so I kept drinking and did nothing. I was working and getting lots of information from colleagues but I couldn't find the courage to do anything useful. I was crippled by shame and guilt and simply buried my feelings and acted as if nothing had happened, but deep down I knew I had a daughter in Falkirk and people were telling me how beautiful she was. I felt heartbroken and paralysed at the same time. 'Should I do the right thing, and ask Susan to marry me? Or should I just ask what she needs from me and try to muddle through somehow?' I was truly lost. Torn between my 'catholic duty' and my fear of being forced to live a life that terrified me, living in a council house and spending my whole life working in Larbert Hospital. My alcohol and drug use were now more problematic as I tried to avoid the feelings which were generating inside me every day.

A few months later and the pain I felt could no longer be sedated. I was obsessed with wanting to do the right thing; getting to know my child and facing up to my responsibilities like a man, I made the decision, fuelled with a large portion of 'Dutch Courage', to call Susan and tell her how I felt. I don't remember the inarticulate clumsy words I used but I tried to apologise for my absence over the last few months and asked if we could try and see if we would work as a couple. Susan was very pragmatic and asked many questions before agreeing that we could see how things went. She gave me all the news on Clare which made me feel better and we arranged to meet up. The next evening, she came through to stay in Denny with Clare. I remember seeing this beautiful little girl crawling around the floor in disbelief that she belonged to me, simply because I didn't feel worthy. I also looked at Susan, for whom I had held such platonic love over the years and who I prayed I could love enough for us to succeed as a couple.

As the weeks progressed and the news got out that we were together and had a child I stopped feeling shame and began to feel pride for the first time. I was proud that I was trying to do what was best and that we could build a life together. My sexuality had never been addressed so I believed that it would just stay dormant and never be spoken of. You can't miss what you've never had as they say, eventually that was to be proven untrue.

Susan's mum and dad welcomed me into their home and made no issue of what had happened up until now. They made a sitting room specifically for us in the back room off the kitchen and furnished it with a small sofa and television. We were able to spend time as a family in the back room, however, like my own parents having separate bedrooms was the catholic norm, so I had to share a bedroom with the boys when I stayed over. I have some very happy memories of those times in Hallglen, when some evenings, Margaret would tell us to go to The Cottages and have a drink together and she would look after Clare. We also spent time in Denny and introduced Clare to lots of her relatives. I don't remember feeling consciously unhappy at that time, but I was again drinking excessively and staying out on benders. I was also working full time in the hospital and working late nights in Denny pubs to make ends meet so I was very busy.

I remember being at a special night-out for someone at Chequers in Hallglen, which was a bit of nightclub where cabaret acts would appear, and food was served as part of the evening. There was a huge table with a lot of my nursing colleagues present, and it was a lovely night with dancing and laughter. I was also smoking Pakistani black cannabis outside in a doorway and was pretty mashed, but I was loving everyone and having a great time. As the crowd dispersed at the end of the night, our friend Moira Freer was dropping Susan home and then taking me home to Denny. I got out of the car to see Susan into the house, not realising that Moira had an inclination of what was about to happen.

Susan and I were leaning against the garage when she said,

"I need to talk." She was then extremely honest and mature about her feelings and her realisation that I was not happy, and that we should break up. I was shocked and pleaded with her that I could be happy; that I just wasn't used to being responsible, that I was immature, and that I could change. She remained very strong and determined in her response and said, "We need to do this, it's the only way." And she left me alone to get back in the car with Moira for the journey home. I cried like a baby all the way home and I could see the panic on Moira's face as this behaviour was unheard of from me. She tried to console me but all I could think of was life without her and Clare and how impossible that felt and my body almost convulsed with my grief. Moira stopped at my house and sat with me until I regained some composure and I went into the house to continue drinking.

Something changed in that moment; I felt broken and unable to recover. I felt immense shame that I had fucked it up and had lost the opportunity to be a father and a husband. My sexuality wasn't even part of the equation at that point, as I had been ignoring it so fiercely. I didn't know what I was going to do or how I was going to get over the feelings I had. As time passed and my drinking escalated again, I became angry, bitter and resentful. Self-pity filled my hours and I blamed everyone else for my situation. I drank and partied like hell, pretending I was ok with everything. I disappeared on benders and no-one knew where I went. I didn't care. When I was challenged I said, "Aw fuck off!" and slammed the door behind me as I walked away. During one of these benders, when I was staying with my friend Janette in Church Walk, I went missing in action for about a week; not even going to work, just trying to forget everything that I was feeling.

Janette could always make me laugh so she was the person I

headed for when I was feeling sad. She would give me the biggest kiss and cuddle and say, "Watch out, Denny. Here we fuckin' come!" as we headed out to the pubs.

It was in one of those pubs that my brother approached me and said, "Where the fuck have you been? Mam's worried sick aboot ye! She's being told about your shenanigans by other people, and you need tae sort it oot!"

This challenge made me even angrier, and I said, "Aw whit the fuck does she care! She's just worrying about the gossips, not about me! She can fuckin' do one an' all!" My binge continued for a few more days before I looked at Janette and said, "I think it's time I went up the road." We both nodded, and I gave her a big squeeze before heading up to Overton Crescent to face Alice.

"Aw yer back" was the greeting I was met with.

"Look Al, dinny start oan me!" I said in the hope that she would back off, but I didn't need to.

She said, "Michael, I can see you're hurting but what you're doing isn't helping you; it's making things worse, so you need to think of another way." She left me alone to read a letter that my mum had delivered, with the instruction 'to be given on his return'.

The envelope was thick, so I knew she had packed a few pages into it. 'Holy fuck,' I thought as I considered the best way forward. I decided to go and sit on the toilet whilst I read the letter as I assumed it would be full of shit. I began to read the first page,

Dear Michael, I am writing this to you as nobody has seen you for weeks and so many people who love you are worried sick about you...

I didn't expect her to be coming from this angle, it took me completely by surprise and it worked. I was blinded by tears in a matter of seconds as I read the pleading, but also honest and supportive letter. She told me to get my act together and if I was so unhappy to move away and start again somewhere else. She suggested that my life in Denny, whether with Susan or not, was doomed from the start as I was doing nothing constructive, only drinking. She addressed my career and how I was going to lose my job.

She spoke about my friends Pat and Brian, how I was letting them down by not being there when they needed me. I sobbed as I read and re-read every page suddenly feeling loved and cared-for. My mum who could never physically say the words that she had written, had composed a letter that shook me back to my feet and made me re-think my life. My lifeline and inspiration to change had come from the person I least expected to understand me: my mum.

I loved my mum very much, but my relationship with her was, at times, complicated. Years of therapy taught me that she did her best and I don't disagree with that, but sometimes her best was not great. Her mother died when she was only young, which must have been awful for the whole family at the time. It was a different world where people had to just get on with it! Grief and loss were acceptable, but only for a limited period of time; otherwise it could be seen as indulgence. I believe that my mum had to close-down her feelings at a young age, which made managing feelings difficult for her later in life. I remember her once saying to me during a heated discussion about feelings, "I canny afford to have feelings, if I start to cry, I might never stop!" It says a lot about how she contained her emotions. I would say that this was not uncommon for the time as many women were also widowed due to two world wars. I knew many relatives and neighbours who had single-handedly brought up families after getting The Telegram. This level of trauma was often handed-down unknowingly onto my generation. My childhood was filled with imagery, history and conversations about 'The War' and it was never far from the surface. I have memories of lying in my bunk-bed worried about dying in a world war.

But I was about to find out an important lesson, that leaving and moving somewhere else doesn't solve anything because you can't run away from yourself.

St Lawrence's

You choose the life you live. If you don't like it, it's on you to change it because no one else is going to do it for you.
—Kim Kiyosaki

Following the explosive letter from my mum, I did what I became pretty good at doing; I pulled myself together and sorted myself out. I went back to work and once again started functioning although I was still avoiding any painful feelings around Susan and Clare and was drinking a fair amount of alcohol at night and over the weekends. Despite this, I was very unhappy and found it almost unbearable to be continually feeling so much anger and sadness about my situation. Although 1981 is not so long ago, was a very different time, there was still a major stigma around having children outside of marriage and I knew many people who'd had shotgun weddings and were very unhappy in their lives. It is difficult to look back with today's knowledge and say what I should have done because there was no road-map through my issue. I felt that the only way to move forward was to move away. I had planned it and thought about it over the years but suddenly it seemed like a good solution. My head told me, crazy as it was that, 'Out of sight, out of mind,' was my only way of coping at that moment.

My friend Margaret Hannah had moved down to Surrey a few months previously, so I called her up to see what the job situation was like. St Lawrence's was a huge 1200 bed Victorian hospital, originally called the London Asylum. It was situated in Caterham on the hill, right next door to the Barracks of the Coldstream Guards. Directly opposite was a pub called The Caterham Arms which had been bombed by the IRA because it was a squaddies pub. Following our conversation, I applied for a charge nurse position; not thinking I would get it at twenty two years old, but I did and within a short space of time I arrived in Surrey and was living in the nurses home.

I was charge nurse on a ward called Wellington E2 which was situated on the male side of the massive, three storey, H-shaped building. The male side was called Wellington and the female Chaldon. My ward had thirty-five long-term patients with a variety of conditions which meant they were a handful. Due to a lack of staffing or inadequate training over many years, the management strategy had been to 'contain' their behaviours which included violence, aggression and serious self-harm. At any given moment of the day there were always several people screaming at the top of their lungs; several biting and scratching each other, and several others smashing windows and furniture. To walk into a ward like that from the street, with no prior experience, would have scared you half to death. It was a tough and relentless job for everyone, but being so young, with my 'pretty boy' looks and trying to be assertive with a tired and jaded team of staff who had worked there for many years was a major task, although at that time I did relish the challenge.

St Lawrence's had extensive grounds with an array of wards and departments scattered over the site. These included a few modern bungalows which had been built for several residents following a Blue Peter appeal. Joey Deacon, who was a long-term patient, had written a book called Tongue Tied about his experience which brought much needed funding and positive attention to the hospital.

A few months prior to my arrival, World in Action had gained undercover access under the guise of being from a university where they wanted to capture episodes of challenging behaviour that they could use for teaching purposes. On the wards, the staff did what they were asked and cooperated as much as possible by standing back for as long as it was safe so that the cameramen could capture the acute moments of extreme behaviour. As soon as there was any risk to the patient or others, they intervened and contained the situation. They believed that by doing so, psychologists would study the footage and devise new management techniques to improve the quality of life of the individuals involved. When the documentary was shown on ITV it had deliberately been shot in a dark sinister light and all of the behaviours which they had filmed were framed in the negative scenario that despite the efforts of these poor people to get attention through their behaviours, the staff stood back and did not intervene. The effect on nursing morale was devastating and there was a sense of grief and sadness among the many staff who had dedicated their lives to doing the best job they could under shocking conditions. The hospital system was far from perfect and there were many areas which could have benefitted from investment and training, but to tar all staff with the same brush had a very destructive effect. My appointment as charge nurse was probably directly due to the negative impact of this programme and made me want to help to change things.

The Hospital Social Club was, without doubt, the most important building in the grounds It was a staff-only members club where they held pay-day dances, cabarets, parties and other events. It was open all day and up till eleven at night and was accessed with an electronic key-card. In the early '80s it was commonplace for working people to have an alcoholic drink with their lunch and then return to work in the afternoons and this was a regular occurrence in the social club.

Living in the nurses home and not knowing a single soul except Margaret who lived a couple of miles away was difficult; so I used to sit in my room with the door ajar, playing my cassette recorder, hoping that someone would knock on the door and start a conversation as they passed by. I was a bit 'stand-offish' and by the third night I decided to front it out and go to the social club on my own. I put my key-card in the slot and it opened, so in I went to the large bar where the functions were held. The club was a cavernous, pre-fabricated building with a small lounge to the left and a huge function suite to the right where most staff gathered. There was a central dancefloor area surrounded by small round Formica tables and bright orange plastic stacking chairs, so it was far from glamorous. It was sparse and had large windows on all sides. There were different groups of people from different wards and departments all sitting in groups drinking and chatting. A juke box played in the background and a few heavy drinking regulars such as the infamous Lynn Savage, stood at the large bar and chatted to everyone who came up for drinks. Lynn was one of the characters I was soon to discover. She was quite masculine and frightened a lot of people with her attitude and, at times, aggressive tone but underneath she was a pussy cat and would do anything for anyone.

The Barman nodded to me and I asked for a pint of lager. As he poured it, I could see the regulars standing at the bar looking at me and I got the odd smile. Lynn Savage came right up to me and said in a loud Cockney accent, "Well who do we have here then? Hello, Darling, my name is Lynn and I'm a cleaner over in the hospital!" She reminded me of my friend Janette from Denny. Fearless yet loyal and often misunderstood.

I said, "I'm Mike and I've just started as a charge nurse on E2." I put my hand out to shake her hand, but she brushed it aside and kissed me right on the lips. "Welcome, Mike!" she roared as she hugged me. Within a few minutes she had loudly introduced several different people to me, clearly aware of how I must be feeling and trying to help me settle in. As different people came to the bar she would say, "Have you met Mike? He's Scottish and just started. Be nice to him!" I did love Lynn Savage!

One of these introductions was a Scottish student nurse called George and his girlfriend Pauline who were sitting with a group of other students at a nearby table. They invited me to join them, which was a lovely gesture, so I dragged over another orange chair and sat down. I very quickly felt relaxed and sat chatting openly, listening and gathering stories about the hospital and the dos and don'ts if I wanted to stay the course in St Lawrence's! George was a former soldier and sat to my right. I don't think he had heard a Scottish accent for a while so was enjoying asking me questions and listening to my broad Scottish responses.

"Fuck, I've not heard that expression for years!" he would say every so often as he threw his head back in loud laughter. "Oh, it's great to meet ye, Mike, I think you're gonna settle in fine," he said as he patted my shoulder. "We're just waiting for Frank who's been home for a few days but he's meeting us here. You'll like him, he's lovely. He's gay and has a boyfriend in the North of England but he's doing his training and stays here most of the time. He lives in the nurses home as well!" he said, unaware of the impact of his words.

My thoughts began to race. Oh God, I was about to meet my

first gay man who lived in the same building as me and maybe he would want to be my friend? There were so many things I wanted to ask him. I had never told a living being that I was gay but maybe tonight would be the first time that I did. My body became anxious, wondering how I would feel when I met him. The only gay men I had ever known were a couple of older men in my hometown who were pitied more than anything else, they were the butt of most of the jokes so I really didn't know what to expect. In hindsight, I applaud them for their courage and honesty.

Around ten p.m. the door opened, and there carrying a rucksack and wearing a smart dark overcoat and a camel scarf, stood Frank. He came over to the table and started to hug everyone and chat. "This is Mike," said George. "He's living in the nurses home and is a charge nurse on E2."

"I'm very pleased to meet you," said Frank, in a friendly way. "What room are you in? I'm room fourteen," he said with a smile.

Feeling quite terrified I said, "Fuck, I'm room eleven, only three doors away!" He sat down next to me and had about ten conversations at once, trying to catch up with everyone.

He was a good-looking lad, a bit of a perfectionist by the look of him, fair hair with a nice haircut and a short beard and moustache. I was shocked at how open he was and that nobody cared about his sexuality. They loved him for who he was. This was a totally new experience for me after spending my life absorbing homophobia from every direction. A gay man who was comfortable in his skin. I was almost dumfounded.

I was terrified and also very sure that I didn't want anyone else in the company to know about me at that point, so I didn't feel able to ask him anything too obvious at the table. I sat staring at him while he chatted and laughed, admiring his courage and strength, fearful of his confidence, curious as to how he had become so self-assured. At one point I was briefly left alone with Frank. I looked around then looked at him in what must have been a desperate, secretive sort of way and said, "Listen, Frank. I'm really glad I met you tonight and I wonder if you could do me a favour? Can I meet you in my room or your room later? I really need to talk to someone and I think I can trust you."

"Oh, Mike," he replied, "I've been travelling all day since I left Howard this morning and I'm really tired, but I'm sure I can stay awake for half an hour and give you a listening ear."

In my dark closet, I was terrified to be seen walking back with him in case anyone thought I was gay, so, like a news of The World reporter, I made my excuses and left, asking him to give me a knock when he got back and I would come along to his room. "Yeah, no problem," he said. "See you in a bit!" I ran through the corridors like electricity was flowing through my body, heading back to the nurses home. I got to my room and looked at myself in the mirror. I put Yazoo on my tape deck and listened to Only You until I heard the heavy fire-door in the corridor bang closed. There was a little knock on my door and a voice quietly said, "Mike, it's Frank. I've got some vodka if you fancy a quick drink?"

"Oh yes please!" I replied, "I'll be along in two minutes!"

I sat on the side of my bed with a rollercoaster of feelings racing through my body. I was terrified. My upbringing told me he must be a bad person and I should stay away from him but my whole being admired his courage and ability to be who he was. I was also frightened that he might try something and, I had never had any sexual contact with a man, I didn't know how I would feel or react should anything like that happen. I had too many fears and anxieties rushing through my body to make any sensible plans for what I needed to do in this moment. I would just have to face my fears and be honest about my feelings and everything would be OK. I stood up to go and quickly sat down again, shaking with nerves like a child at Xmas. Not knowing how to handle this situation as it wasn't in my rule book. Finally, I walked the short distance to his room.

He had been living there for a little while, so his room was much nicer and more homely than mine, with nice artwork and modern kitchen appliances. I had very little as I had only just moved down, so I was immediately embarrassed when I thought of my room. "This is lovely, Frank," I said as I entered the room.

"Grab a seat on the bed," he said, "I have got ice here somewhere."

The standard rooms back then did not have much space and only had a bed; a sink, a chest of drawers and a wardrobe. He had cleverly fitted in a small fridge and a shelf unit which held his kettle and toaster. I sat on the single bed, which was against the window wall, facing the door. Frank handed me a vodka and lemonade, with ice, and sat down towards the bottom of the bed, a safe distance I noted.

"So, what can I help you with, Mike?" he said in a really calm and caring voice. I became very uncomfortable, glugged half of my drink down and took a breath. "I've never told anyone this, and I've got a daughter in Scotland so I don't know if it's true, but I get these feelings and thoughts and, sometimes I wonder if I might be like you?" I couldn't have been clumsier if I had tried!

"So, what's making you think that, Mike, if you've been sleeping with girls up until now?" he replied in a somewhat curious tone.

"Well, that's what I mean." I protested. "I've never had the opportunity before, the place I come from near Glasgow is not like that and I couldn't talk to anyone about it, so I've carried these feelings for years. Besides, lots of people called me gay and sissy when I was younger, so maybe I went with women to prove I wasn't, I just don't fuckin' know!" I said as I became quite breathless and agitated by my ramblings. Frank gently moved a little closer to me and put his hand reassuringly on my arm. I thought I was going to scream at the sensation which immediately rushed through my body. Physical contact, tenderness from a male. Not a slap or a punch or a poke. A gentle touch. I felt my body begin to shake as if I was shivering. What the fuck was going on!

As he leaned-in towards me slowly I panicked and said, "What are you doing?"

He looked me directly in the eyes and, in a low sexy voice said, "We're gonna find out if you're gay, that's what we're gonna do." His head gently tilted and came forward as his lips met mine in a tender, warm and beautiful kiss. It lasted a very long time and I really didn't want it to end. It was the most beautiful sensation. He slowly pulled his head back and whispered, "How was that?" I couldn't find the words. I felt very emotional, almost overwhelmed, so I just smiled at him and moved my head back for another kiss.

Things progressed and slowly we undressed each other and got into bed. We made love every different way we could think of, for hours, laughing and chatting between each passionate segment, lying together, embracing, touching, oblivious to anything else which was happening outside of that room. Two people, in the moment, loving each other. I knew in that moment who I truly was and I felt indestructible. In the morning we had coffee, chatted and laughed for a while and then he went to work. "Just pull the door behind you when you go, Mike. Thank you for last night, it was very special," he said, and he kissed me goodbye.

I remember sitting smiling to myself, still caught up in the amazing feelings of the night before, replaying moments in my head. I then remember suddenly hearing someone walk along the corridor outside of the room and I was immediately filled with the shame I was used to. Who did I think I was? Everybody was going to find out about this and then where would I be? I sneaked along the corridor back to my room and showered before going on a late shift. As I walked along the wide corridors to Wellington block, I truly thought that everyone knew what I had been doing. Every look or smile made me believe that they were in the know. The familiar negative thoughts and feelings I was used to, returned to their comfortable place within me and I felt dirty and ashamed.

When I got into work things weren't so bad, I managed to stop feeling ashamed as I focused on my job, which I was good at. My shift finished at ten p.m. and I headed straight back to my room. I closed the door behind me and sat on the bed feeling a strange mixture of happiness, fear and my ongoing shame attack me.

I hadn't even taken off my unform when the gentle knock came at the door and Frank unexpectedly arrived. "How was your day?" he asked as he handed me a drink and asked if I wanted a sandwich. "I had a busy day," he said as he sat on my bed. There was a sudden silence and he looked right at me as I pulled on a tee shirt. "I've been thinking about you all day, Mike Delaney," he said, as if feeling surprised and guilty. "And I don't know what that means."

I was confused by everything and said, "Frank, my head is fucked after last night. I spent the day hiding, thinking everyone knew my business. I've felt deliriously happy one minute, followed by moments of absolute terror wondering who you've told the next. I don't know if I can do this stuff," I said assertively, although I felt far from assertive.

"What do you mean?" he said, "You didn't enjoy last night?"

"Oh, Frank," I responded, "You have absolutely no idea how much I loved last night. I am twenty-two years old and have had many thoughts in my head about how my first encounter with a man could feel, but none of them could ever come close to what I experienced last night. It was unforgettable, but the fallout today for me has been huge."

He looked puzzled and said, "Tell me what you mean."

"Are you a Catholic?" I asked in a sarcastic tone.

"Oh Jesus no!" he said with a laugh.

"In that case you wouldn't understand," I said and sat beside him on the bed. "What about Howard?" I asked in a bid to move the focus away from me.

"What about him?" came the uncaring response.

I knew they had been together for several years and that this was serious. I did not want to be responsible for wrecking his relationship plus I was beginning to drown in shame just by talking about the events of last night, yet a part of me felt free and happy. How can so many extremes of emotions, both positive and negative, exist at the same time? He sat close to me and handed me my drink. He then laid his head against my shoulder and said, "Mike Delaney, I think I've fallen in love with you. I didn't expect or plan it, but it's happened, and it's made me rethink everything. I'm not expecting you to have the same feelings as me but that's ok. We can see how things go. Whatever happens, I'm not going back to Howard."

It's difficult to convey how I felt in that moment. I didn't want to be responsible for him ending his relationship, but at that moment I felt like I had fallen in love with him as well. In twenty-four hours every single aspect of who I was felt like it had shifted. I hadn't said it out loud yet, but I knew for sure I was gay. I was terrified by that admission, yet I looked at him and felt safe and secure, maybe for the first time ever. He kept telling me how beautiful and special I was, how lucky he felt to have met me and that he would not put any pressure on me. I kept thinking of the life I had left and how I would be rejected completely if anyone found out about this. An inner conflict raged as I tried to feel comfortable when I knew I was going against everything that I had been taught, but the stubborn, angry part of me wanted to tell the world. I shared some of what I was feeling and said to Frank, "This is all new to me. You will have to be patient. Within twenty-four hours I've come out, had a night of amazing sex and now you're telling me you are leaving your partner. I can't handle all this at once! Last night at this time I thought I was straight!" I added as a closing line with some humour but as quick as a flash he came back with "No-one was ever going to believe that story, love!" which made me laugh from my belly! We laid together and his presence stopped me from feeling frightened.

St Lawrence's Continued

One of the hardest things was learning that I was worthy of recovery.

Following my initial encounter with Frank, he did end his relationship with Howard and we became good friends (sometimes with benefits). He was very protective of me and only ever wanted to shield me from the negative elements of the gay scene, as I looked younger than my years and did not know how to navigate my way around a risky, underground scene. At times I found his care and concern somewhat controlling and smothering, but I also knew and appreciated that it was coming from a good place and that he was trying to educate me in new ways of surviving. Being gay was still not an accepted lifestyle choice and was about to become a whole lot worse due to the arrival of AIDS.

Caterham was only a few miles from Croydon and had a small scene which consisted of one pub called The Croydon, which was tucked up a side street, and a club that had one evening per month in The Greyhound. I had been nagging Frank to go out and see the gay scene as I had never experienced it. He wasn't really a 'scene queen' but he finally agreed to go out with me on a Friday evening. We got the bus into Croydon around seven p.m. and went into The Croydon for an early drink. It was quite a big and fairly modern pub with a spiral staircase in the middle which went downstairs to a smaller bar area. The rest of it was low-lighting with groups of men, single men standing around, hoping to be picked-up by someone. I was a bit apprehensive about this and Frank said, "Don't you dare pick anyone up in here, they'll be all over you, 'cos you're new!" He was right. It was very claustrophobic and everywhere I stood I was being winked at or beckoned for a drink. After a while I got bored with it and suggested we go to the club. We arrived at the Greyhound and knocked on the door, a bit like the prohibition venues in a gangster movie. It was a knock three times and ask for Benny, type of place. We got inside and it was really a large function suite with the dancefloor in the middle surrounded by tables. I half expected the bride and groom to arrive for the first dance!

As the night went on and the high-energy music began to boom it came to life. It got fairly busy with new people, some of whom I had seen in The Croydon. The dancefloor got busy and there were some really good dancers. I stopped for a minute and watched the exhibition on the dancefloor and was really impressed by the peacock displays as people outdid each-others' moves and upped the standard every few minutes. It was also the first time I had seen the 'fan-dancers' who were usually buff and dressed quite masculinely with jeans and checked shirts but who held a large fan in each hand and used them to do some interesting 'armography' as they say nowadays on Strictly. There were a few men in full leather gear including cowboy chaps and leather hats adorned by chains and a few badly dressed drag queens who looked like they had come straight from Sue Riders' shop window. Between these confident archetypes there were people who felt like me: ordinary blokes who were just trying to find out where and how they fitted-in. I was also struck by the fact that there was not a single woman in the place except for the bar-staff which, for me, was a very strange feeling.

After a few drinks I got up and danced, but it felt awkward. My whole experience previously had been straight nightclubs with the occasional fight, and although I was happy to be in a gay venue, it felt strange. More like a room full of misfits than a confident group of 'out' gay men. Despite being 'cruised' by a few men, I wasn't feeling it and I could also see that Frank was bored too, so I asked if he was ready to go and I could see the relief in his face as he nodded his head and we started heading to the coat check.

As we stepped out into the dark night, Frank said, "If we do a left down here, we should be able to get a taxi quite quickly. The Fairfield Halls are over there so there are usually plenty of drivers looking for a fare." As we walked along, I suddenly heard noises coming from across the busy main road.

"Fucking queers! You dirty fuckin' poofters!" was being screamed at us by a group of four or five young men who were running on the other side of the road trying to catch up with us. Luckily it was a busy dual carriageway so they couldn't run straight over. We started to run, praying that a taxi would show up and save us. "We're gonna fuckin' kill you, you queer bastards!" came bellowing across the noisy traffic as we sped-up our pace to keep ahead of them.

I caught sight of them starting to cross the traffic and get to the central barriers and, just at that point, a black taxi pulled in and the driver said, "Where to?"

We both jumped in the back seat and Frank said, "Caterham please, and hurry 'cos those guys are after us!"

The driver quickly pulled away and said, "Fucking toerags! You just come out of The Greyhound then?" as if it was a normal occurrence.

"Yes," said Frank, "I didn't expect that kind of thing coming out of there at night."

The driver looked at us in the rear-view mirror and said, "Some people are fuckin' stupid, mate! They don't like anything that they don't understand. My oldest is gay and, until it came into my life, I was pretty much like them in my attitude." "Live and let live I say!" he added in an unexpectedly supportive way as we drove towards Purley, relieved to have escaped a potentially dangerous situation. That's when I realised that, even the open and cosmopolitan areas of Greater London had their share of intolerant haters and I would have to be careful about where I went and what I did.

The following week I sat down and had a chat with Frank as I could see he was in a lot of emotional pain around our relationship and where it was going. I could sense his strong feelings for me and, although I loved him as a friend and enjoyed being with him, I knew that I wasn't 'in love' with him. I could feel his protectiveness begin to develop into controlling behaviours and I didn't know what the best way forward was so I felt that honesty would be the best policy. I told him how I felt and that I loved him but that I didn't feel I could give him the long-term relationship that he was hoping for. He was very upset and asked if I could continue as things were until I was sure, but I told him that I was sure and that I was becoming unhappy that I was hurting him in the process. He was very upset and tearful, which, in turn made me cry too, so I held him and whispered in his ear how sorry I was, we both cried together for a while before he said goodnight and returned to room fourteen.

Within a week and without any warning, Frank disappeared. Unbeknown to me, he had met with the administrators for the nursing school and resigned from his position. According to George who I met in the social club, he had returned to Howard in Yorkshire and had given up nursing. I felt devastated that I had caused him so much pain and that he was unable to continue his training. The guilt I felt was palpable and became heightened if I bumped into any of his friends. George was very upset and blamed me for his departure, saying that I fucked with his head and suggested I had played games, which I absolutely had not. In fact, I was probably more open and honest with Frank than I had ever been in any relationship. I was conscious of hurting him and tried every way not to do that, but I could not be responsible for his feelings. I knew in my heart that I had not used or manipulated him, and I didn't like the implications that I had.

Soon after that I was in work and happened to be collecting some of my patients from the adventure playground which was situated on site and consisted of different activity areas and an animal corner with a donkey and chickens. As I entered the gate I was approached by a tall, handsome young man who said, "Can I help you?"

"I've come to collect Jacob and Martin from E2," I said with a smile. He returned the smile and had a look in his eye which was new to me and made me curious.

I wasn't sure what this new body-language meant, so I stayed quiet, however he smiled at me again and said, "They're not quite finished, do you fancy a quick coffee?"

Surprised at the offer I said, "Yes, please." He beckoned me to follow him into the office area. We sat down together with our drinks and he was very open and friendly. His style was very trendy, and his clothing was not regular chain-store items but more designer than I had ever seen. His name was Mark and he lived in nearby Kenley with his partner Andrew. We sat for a little while and chatted very politely.

I could tell he was gay but was not sure if he knew I was until he said, "Is it you that was seeing Frank?" I was shocked at that statement and didn't know how to respond.

"Eh, yes," I replied as I began to drown in shame and headed for the gate.

"You'll have to come over for dinner one evening," he said as I collected my two charges. "I'll phone you on the ward and let you know a good time," he said as I walked away from the gates.

"That would be lovely. Thanks, Mark!" I replied. I walked back to the ward stunned that people knew my business before they had even met me.

About a week later I was picked up from the hospital by Mark and Andrew and driven the four or five miles to Kenley where dinner was almost ready to serve. As I entered the front door, I almost let out a gasp, their house was stunning. Although small, it had been made with an open plan so downstairs was a huge lounge with a spiral staircase going upstairs, and just through a small arch was an extension which housed a very modern kitchen and bathroom. The furniture and fixtures were some of the most unusual, and expensive looking things, I had ever seen outside of a magazine shoot. I was mightily impressed. Dinner was very pleasant, and it was nice getting to know them both. They had been together for a few years and had met through the lonely-hearts section in Time-Out Magazine, which I suppose was the internet dating of its time.

Andrew was older and quite successful in his business. He also played rugby on the weekends and, it transpired, was very much in the closet as his conservative family and work colleagues could never accept his sexuality.

"How does that work for you, Mark?" I asked curiously.

"Oh, if his friends or family visit, they think I'm the lodger," he replied with a laugh. I couldn't help but think that this must be difficult for him to manage, living a nice life but having to pretend to be the lodger. In my mind it almost made the act of coming out less meaningful, if he was still having to deny who he was.

Andrew was a good bit older and was short, heavy-set and balding; very much a rugby player in appearance. He seemed very generous and enjoyed being in charge, but also seemed to like the power which that brought. The way he spoke was very intellectual, often trying to suss me out and see how educated and politically aware I was. I was more than a match for him intellectually, but I could almost feel the emerging challenge of having to fight off his advances as he was very suggestive; always following with a touch against my leg as he laughed. I didn't dislike him, but I was very wary as he felt a bit sleekit, as we say in Scotland.

As the evening got late and we began to drink brandy and liqueurs I started to think it was about time I was getting home. "I really should be going, Andrew. It's getting late and I'm working tomorrow," I said, knowing that I was in the middle of nowhere and was depending on him to drive me home.

"Oh, didn't Mark say?" he replied, "I've had a drink so we thought you could stay the night and I'll drop you at work in the morning?"

I could feel the possibility that I may have been set-up and could feel the trap tighten, I quickly responded by saying, "Andrew, I can get a taxi, do you have any numbers handy?"

"Oh, you'll never get a taxi at this time of night around here, they're all in Croydon and Purley where the nightclubs are busy," said Andrew.

Then Mark began to join him, "Just stay the night, Mike, we won't bite!" he said with a wry smile on his face. They both stood up from the table and beckoned me to move with them to the leather sofa at the other side of the room. Part of me felt tricked and angry but I didn't want to look innocent and 'uncool,' so I picked up my brandy and cigarettes and sat next to Mark on the sofa while Andrew sat on his designer leather recliner.

Mark put Where is my Man by Eartha Kitt on the record deck and sat back down next to me, but this time a little closer. "Have you ever had a threesome?" asked Andrew in a suggestive tone.

"No, it's not really my scene, Andrew," I said, as if I was experienced in such things but actually feeling terrified of what might be planned for me.

"Don't knock it till you've tried it!" he replied in a determined tone. "It might be right up your street!" I could feel the pincer movement beginning as Mark moved closer to me on the sofa and put his hand on my shoulder. I began to panic as I had no intention of engaging in any acts with a couple; especially when one of them was old, short, bald and fat!

Eventually I was quite direct as their plan was so blindingly obvious that I could no longer ignore it. "Can you show me to the spare room please," I said firmly. "I really don't want to get into this threesome shite so; if you don't mind, I'll go to bed now and I'd be grateful for a lift to the hospital in the morning." My words did the trick and the energy shifted.

"Oh well, it was worth a try, eh, Mark?" said Andrew with a laugh. 'Yeah, I fuckin' bet it was, you old creep,' I thought to myself as I began to relax again; safe in the knowledge that I wasn't about to be gang-banged!

As it turned out they never tried it again, and I became good friends with them both – at one point moving into the house for a short time when a rental property I was staying in fell through. It was when I was living there that Andrew came home early one Friday evening and said, "Right you two, get showered and dressed in your best clothes; we're going into London for the night!" at which point Mark and I jumped up to our feet excitedly.

"Where are we going?" asked Mark. "I need to know so I can decide what to wear!"

"We're going to eat in Croydon first, then I thought we could hit Heaven," he replied. Mark screamed and ran up the spiral staircase to start looking for clothes. "Come on, Mike, you can borrow something if you like," he said, and I quickly followed him up the stairs. I was so excited as I had heard of Heaven through Time-Out Magazine articles; it was known to be the biggest gay club in Europe at that time with various different floors and themed areas.

By eight p.m. we were in a beautiful Italian restaurant in South Croydon, with genuine Italian staff; small tables with blue gingham tablecloths and an incredible menu of things I had never heard of. As Andrew liked to be the 'father figure' of the group, he said, "Let me order for you, I know what's best" which made me nervous.

"Andrew, I don't like smelly fish or prawns in their shells so don't order me anything like that please," I asked.

"Don't worry," he said, "I'll look after you." He then proceeded to speak fluent Italian to the waiter so I was still none the wiser about what he had ordered. We all had gin and tonics and our food began to arrive, different starters which we could share; all presented beautifully in small dishes. "Try this, Mike,"

Andrew would say as he offered me different spiced sausages and meats.

It was truly beautiful, and my taste buds didn't know what had hit them, but when the main course arrived, I said, "What's this? Chicken?" as I looked at a golden brown, breadcrumbed fillet with a small bone sticking out of one end.

"Chicken Kiev," said Andrew smugly, followed by, "Don't touch it till the waiter has opened it." At that point the waiter arrived with a pointed, sharp kitchen knife and proceeded to gently pierce the side of the fillet. There was almost an explosion as steaming hot, garlic and herb butter poured from the incision and began to flood my plate. The smell was like nothing else I had ever smelt, so I chose some vegetables from the dishes in the middle and began to eat the amazing feast.

By the end of the meal, after demolishing a couple of bottles of wine and several brandies, Andrew, who had only had a small amount of alcohol said; "Ok kids, let's go" and we headed back to the car for the half-hour journey into central London. After parking, we arrived at the entrance of Heaven which was not very grand at all just a small frontage in the narrow Villiers Street, close to Embankment Station. After heading down a few stairs from street level there was a small desk where admission fees were paid. It was manned by an outrageous, but amazing, looking drag queen surrounded by an entourage of characters who posed and smiled at the arriving punters.

We walked through a set of double doors and I could feel the thumping vibration of the bass coming from the dancefloor, which was through another set of doors a few feet away. I can still remember opening those doors and walking into this place I had read about, it far exceeded any of my expectations. It was absolutely massive, like an aircraft hangar, with black walls and a ceiling which perfectly showed the amazing display of lasers and lights installed to their full effect. I must have looked like a typical tourist as I stood, with my mouth open, staring at the sight which I beheld. Thousands of gay men of every description danced all over the place wherever I looked. I had gone from Scotland, where I didn't know a single gay man, to this club where I was surrounded by thousands of them. It felt like I had come home. Around the edges of the dancefloor people stood chatting, smoking and taking drugs, which I later discovered were poppers. I had never seen or felt anything like it in my life. I stood still, just staring at everything which was going on around me and felt incredible. This was the gay scene I had been looking for! Fuck the Greyhound in Croydon; this was spectacular!

Andrew and Mark were a bit more accustomed, as they had been here many times, so they said, "Why don't we go upstairs and have a drink?" I nodded in agreement and followed them up a huge black wrought iron staircase which rose from one side of the dancefloor, stopping every so often on a level viewing platform which gave an amazing aerial view of the dancefloor, until it reached a mezzanine floor high above the crowd. Again, we passed through a couple of doors and we were in The Star Bar which had a long, oval shaped bar in the centre of the room, surrounded by different levels of wall seating which were commonly known as The Meat Rack as it was where men hung around if they were looking to be picked up by someone.

This room had a very different vibe and was more of a conversation and meeting place, but it was still full of the most fascinating creations. Human art, in the form of complex costumes, hairstyles and make up; designed to get the full attention of everyone in the place. I just couldn't stop staring at people, so much so that some of them started drawing me dirty looks and sticking their tongues out at me, so I quickly learned to make my fascination more discreet! I looked towards the other end of the room at one point and had to do a double take. I nudged Mark and said, "Is that Boy George?" who had just released Karma Chameleon.

"Oh my God, it is!" said Mark. "Shall we go and talk to him?"

"No!" I screamed over the music, "I wouldn't know what to say! Besides, I've read that he is horrible," I said, not knowing that many years later he would become my friend.

As it turned out a few months into my stay with them Andrew admitted to Mark that he was having an affair with someone else called James, and he was in love with him. Mark was devastated as he did love Andrew, but he had also got used to his comfortable lifestyle, nice clothing, holidays and gifts. I was still surprised at the hysteria which was played out every night with Mark threatening suicide and begging to be taken back. He had come from a poor family in East London and enjoyed the trappings which his relationship brought. Eventually Andrew couldn't bear the drama as it was reaching the ears of his conservative family, so he came up with a plan which would get Mark out of the house while making him less angry and venomous. He paid the deposit and initial rent on a three-bedroomed house in Old Coulsdon for both of us, it was close to work and in a nice neighbourhood. It was a beautiful semi-detached house with an extension on the back.

Needless to say, I loved it and was enthusiastic about the move, but Mark knew that if he moved out it was the definitive end of his relationship, so he was resistant to the offer. When he refused, Andrew lost the plot and said, "I didn't want to do this but, if you don't move out, I will move James into my room, and you will be the lodger!"

Mark screamed at him across the lounge, "You wouldn't fucking dare! I'll burn this fucking house down before I let that prick sleep in my bed!" At that moment Andrew grabbed his car keys and left the house.

"Where are you going?" screamed Mark as he followed him into the street screeching "Don't walk away from me!" but I heard the engine roar and Andrew disappeared out of sight at the end of the road.

Mark was sobbing uncontrollably on the couch. I was feeling incredibly uncomfortable and didn't want to put too much pressure on him about the new house, but I was praying that he would accept as it could be a really good start for us both to be in a nice house. Eventually Mark had cried it all out, so I poured us a couple of strong drinks and sat next to him. "Where do you think he's gone?" he said in a childlike tone.

"I don't know, Mark," I said, "but he sounded angry and determined when he left."

A little while later a car pulled up and the front door was thrown open. "This is James," said Andrew as he ushered a young blonde man into the lounge, followed by his suitcases and some boxes. Mark did not do what I expected him to do. I could see the shock all over his face, but he was unable to react in his usual way because he knew James! Andrew looked at Mark and said, "This is no longer up for discussion, Mark; you can move into the spare room until I sign contracts, but after that you are moving into Lacey Avenue with Mike! If you have any problem with that you can leave now, and I will drop you at a mainline station if you want to go home to East London."

Boom! No more dramas, no more discussions. The decision had been made and the plan had been moved into action. Mark left the room in silence and went upstairs to move his stuff into the spare room. Andrew knew he would never return to his roots as he had gone to so much effort to get away from them. The atmosphere in the house was absolutely electric, like something explosive could happen at any second. James understandably looked very sheepish and sat quietly as the unpredictable situation progressed.

Suddenly Mark appeared at the bottom of the spiral staircase and said, "Anyone for a cup of tea? James?" I could not believe what was happening, Mark was pretending that everything was OK and suddenly had a smile on his face.

"That would be very nice, thank you, Mark," said James in a very Etonian accent and Mark walked through the room to get to the kitchen.

"How are you, James? Long-time no see," he said as he entered the kitchen.

"I'm good; thanks, Mark," said James. I was absolutely stunned by this strange, yet apparently, acceptable behaviour. In Scotland there would have been a fight to the death and one of them would be lying in the street beside their belongings. But here they were 'chit-chatting' like they had just bumped into each other in a chip-shop!

Mark returned with a tray of teas, and some chocolate biscuits, and we all took a cup and sat down. I couldn't bear the fake niceness or the long silences as they both planned their next chess move. "How do you two know each other?" I clumsily asked in an attempt to break the silence.

"Oh, we worked together on a project with horses at St Lawrence's," James replied. "I was Mark's Boss," he said with some delight.

"Yes, but not for long," said Mark. "I don't like being

managed by people who don't have a clue what they are doing," he said. I could almost hear the umpire call "Fifteen love!" as they aimed passive aggressive volleys at each other. It was actually quite entertaining, once you moved past the tragedy. Eventually everything was reasonably calm, and Mark headed upstairs to his new bedroom, deliberately walking slowly up the stairs like Bette Davies. "Goodnight everyone… Sleep well," he said as he disappeared out of view. When we heard the door to his room close Andrew said, "I'll get onto that house tomorrow Mike, sorry you've had to endure all this shit tonight."

"Don't worry, Andrew," I replied, in the full knowledge that I was about to become the tenant in a fully furnished, three-bedroomed semi-detached house in Old Coulsdon. "I'll look after him."

Broadway Patients and Staff

I got to be close to a few people at Broadway during my time in primary care. There was a girl called Vanessa from Birmingham who I got on very well with. She was of mixed heritage and had two young children, however her descent into a full blown crack addiction had gotten social services involved along with the police and their schools. One of the reasons she had gotten funding for rehabilitation was because she held her children hostage until social services agreed to fund her. Although she was a lovely person and great fun to be around; there was a deep shame and sadness which surrounded her. Many nights we sat in the large lounge putting the world to rights, but she really struggled with the concept of abstinence. It seemed her pain was so deep that she could only go for limited periods without sedation to escape from it.

Micky was another character who came in and made me die laughing from day one. He was from a close-knit cockney family and was full of one-liners. He had done several rehabs and struggled with longer term sobriety, so every so often his family would foot the bill for an eight week programme. Underneath his humour and bravado was a lot of wisdom and at times I was surprised at how he would help others, very quietly, in the background. I remained in touch with him for some time afterwards but then I believe he got married and moved to the Southeast of England, and we lost touch.

Lisa was a compulsive overeater and came in from the

Northeast. When she arrived, she was a very large young lady and she shared with me one evening that she used to shop in Makro and bought commercial packs of everything. Her favourite snack was pickled onion Monster Munch and when she sat down to watch TV she would tear open the end of the box containing forty-eight bags and would eat them all in one sitting. She also had an amazing sense of humour and we laughed a lot together. The regime for overeaters was three full meals a day, with nothing between meals, and when she left Broadway she wore a size twelve dress and looked amazing.

There was another girl who was an overeater who really taught me how life-threatening her condition could be. I will call her Melissa and she was a very wealthy and educated young girl who spoke in a very quiet, well-educated accent. I learned after spending some time with her in secondary care that she had substantial childhood trauma which haunted her. She had been doing some trauma work, and one evening when we were all supposed to go out to a fellowship meeting, she said she felt very tired and, if we didn't mind, she wanted to have an early night. None of us felt the need to challenge her and we all left in the minibus for Bristol, but unbeknown to us, she had gathered a stash of cakes, biscuits and sweets, as well as two litre bottles of coke to wash them down. When we returned, we found her semi-conscious and having difficulty breathing. Her speech was slurred, and she seemed almost drunk, it was the effect that consuming so much sugar had had on her. Her difficulty in breathing was because she had eaten so much that her stomach was pushing upwards into her lungs and subsequently they couldn't expand fully when she tried to breathe. In all my years of nursing I had never seen anyone so very ill from just consuming a vast amount of sweet food and drinks. We alerted the staff who had to call an ambulance and have her admitted to a general hospital.

There was a lady called Liz who came into secondary care when I was there. She had done a full treatment through another provider but had relapsed on her return home to Birmingham so was accepted for secondary care. She was a middle-aged woman, with a grown-up family, and had a lovely gentle personality. Once I got to know her, I realised that she had been a victim of domestic abuse for many years, even in her previous rehab her counsellor had become very good friends with her abusive husband, even spending time with him during his visits to the centre. She described waiting to be called into a couple's session and hearing them both laughing loudly before she was invited in. How can you be expected to trust a process when this kind of unprofessional behaviour is allowed to happen? She had become accustomed to the misconception that if she was a drunk, who could blame him for hitting her! When in fact, the drinking had started later; as a means of avoiding the ongoing pain and violence from her husband. Liz did very well, and I stayed in touch with her for years and used to meet her when I lived in Birmingham. She did not return to her husband and had a very happy life on her own and with her children and grandchildren. Sadly, she took ill and passed away a few years ago, but she remained sober and was surrounded by her family.

Darren was a young gay lad from London who was in primary care when I arrived. He was a heroin user but, as is often the case, there was a dark history of childhood trauma underpinning the drug-use. I enjoyed sitting with him in the evenings as he was a good laugh and didn't really get too involved in the dramas of the rehab. He had been in a relationship with an older guy called Russell for a number of years and received regular phone calls, cards and letters from him, as well as weekend visits. Being so far away from my family, I didn't get a single visit during my five-month stay, but I got some beautiful cards and letters from family and friends which I still treasure. We both moved down to secondary care at the same time, so our friendship grew, and I met Russell during his visits.

I will always remember Darren going on about his birthday the previous year and how he had a surprise party and how fabulous it was. He always said, "I'm gonna get Russell to bring down the video, it's so funny, you'll love it!" until eventually, some weeks later, the VHS recording arrived. Darren was so excited and invited everyone in secondary care to come to house four to watch. We all got teas and coffees and sat around the TV as Darren excitedly pressed play on the player and sat down. The first few minutes were of people arriving and Darren telling us who they were, then he said excitedly, "Oh, the camera's going inside now, you'll have a laugh!" but as the camera followed guests into the large lounge, the first thing we were greeted with was Darren sitting on the couch 'gouching out' on heroin! The cameraman then tried to make things look better by chatting with the crowd and watching people dancing, but every time he went near one side of the room, you were always able to see Darren unconscious in the background. It was a very sad and uncomfortable moment until Darren said, "Oh for fuck's sake, turn that off!" before running to the toilet in tears. We all felt for him as it could have been any one of us in that situation.

After I had left treatment, and was living in Blackthorn Gardens in Worle, he called me to let me know that he was using again.

"Could I come and stay with you for a bit while I detox?" he asked.

"But of course, Darren," I replied, "I'll get you out to meetings and stuff and we can have a laugh."

He arrived the next day with an initial attitude of positivity and motivation, but when his withdrawals started to kick-in he struggled. I had managed to get him an emergency appointment at my GP surgery so he had some Valium to help him, but it wasn't helping. He had been using much more than he had admitted including large amounts of Valium, he was in a lot of pain. One day I had to go out to pick up a new bike I had bought from a shop in Weston so before I left I knocked on the bedroom door to see how he was. I told him that I wouldn't be long, and that I would do us some food when I got back. He said he felt OK and would stay in bed, so I left. I got back a couple of hours later to find my front door lying wide open, Darren was nowhere to be seen. I called his name and went upstairs to see if he was there, but that was when I saw the place in a mess; with my possessions scattered around and my large suitcase missing. I checked further and there was some money and a few other things missing. Whilst I understood why he had done it, I was still angry that he had chosen that option instead of talking to me. My neighbours told me later that day that a taxi had arrived, and he had run 'like lightning' with my large case and disappeared in seconds. I never saw or heard from Darren again, but I would still have forgiven and supported him if I had. One of the many things I have learned about addictions is to try and look beyond the behaviour and deal with the illness. The person we love is still in there, underneath all these destructive behaviours.

Andy was a middle-aged man from Devon who came in to stop his drinking. Initially he was a troubled, angry man who seemed to actually be frightened a lot of the time, but it was easier and more effective to show anger as his default setting. He was the first person whom I ever observed completely change as he understood and trusted the process. He went from being an intimidating, aggressive man to a pussy-cat in a matter of weeks. He became so happy that he had found recovery that he had a smile on his face for most of the day. The counsellors warned him that he was on 'the pink cloud' and that everything could change very quickly, however it didn't change before he left and, when I met him at reunions, he was still the happy man I had gotten to know in primary treatment. He used to say to people, "You can't upset me 'cos I'm in a state of grace." It always made me laugh as it came from one of the books we had to read.

The Staff

Never be bullied into silence. Never allow yourself to be made a victim. Accept no one's definition of your life; define yourself.
—Harvey Fierstein

When I arrived in Broadway, the CEO was a strong lady called Diana who ran a very tight, and disciplined, ship. We used to hear about the six-minute warning; which was the time you were given to pack your belongings and get into a waiting taxi, if you broke the rules and were ejected from treatment, most commonly when illicit drugs or alcohol were used. There were very clear rules, with very clear consequences, so the modus operandi of Broadway was that if you broke the rules, it was a choice that you made and therefore you had to face the consequences of your actions even if it meant ending your treatment. It was effective for people like me who were used to operating well under those kinds of rules but for many people, those with chaotic and traumatic pasts, it was very difficult to suddenly become organised and disciplined.

The nursing team was led by Pauline, who was soon to become CEO for many years and to steer Broadway from financial insecurity onto solid ground. She also became a very good friend and supported me in many ways when I was setting up and developing new services. She also managed a tight ship, amongst the nurses, whilst I was there, getting something as simple as paracetamol was a major operation. The policy was to talk about your feelings rather than take a drug, and for the most part it was successful as I observed on many occasions. The nursing department held a gentler energy than the counselling department however there were no caretakers in the team. They had been trained well, to explore every option before giving out any unnecessary medications, which included remedies like Indian head massage for the ever-present headaches, and Sony Walkmans, which played whale song if you couldn't sleep! We weren't allowed real music but the sharper patients would say that they couldn't sleep so that they could get the Walkman then they would swap out the whale song for their own cassette so when the nurses did a check it looked settled. Only when someone had the music so loud that it could be heard rattling out of the headphones would suspicion be aroused.

Most of the counselling team were in recovery themselves so were passionate about their work. They worked to the same boundaries and managed groups firmly, and within agreed guidelines. The rules and expectations of treatment were extensive and tightly adhered to. This included rules around no music, no TV, no newspapers, and no exclusive relationships within treatment. The philosophy was that all of these things were distractions from the work you needed to do, although, with hindsight, I feel that maybe the complete ban on these things made them harder to manage when treatment was over. My focal counsellor was called Stefan and he did some really good work with me in primary. In secondary care I worked with Graham who, although very strict and direct, worked with me in a very challenging but supportive way, which I really appreciated, as I don't respond well to coercion or bullying.

There were also a number of students who came on training placements for several weeks or months at a time. One of these students was a lady called Chris who had been homeless on the streets of London for many years before finding recovery and writing a very successful book. I found her inspiring and fascinating as she had climbed from the lowest position you can find yourself in. A few months later I met her in an AA meeting where she had just done an amazing share about her experience, strength and hope where she made sleeping rough sound beautiful, as she had had a long-term relationship with a homeless ballet dancer. Whilst chatting over a coffee, I asked, "Chris, what was the catalyst, after so many years on the street, that made you fight for recovery?"

I saw a smile appear on her face and she said, "You probably won't believe this." Before going on to say, "It was a cold winter night, and I was on my own sleeping in a shop doorway in Oxford Street, when I was startled by what I thought was water pouring over me. When I opened my eyes, I was shocked to realise that a uniformed policeman was pissing on me! At that moment I thought, if the people who are supposed to ensure my safety were treating me like this, what was the point? So the very next day I went to an addiction service and asked for help." Apart from a successful book, she had also gained a degree at John Moore's University in Liverpool. Quite a lady!

One of the counsellors whom I also admired was a gentle lady called Elizabeth who was very empathic and compassionate in the way she worked. I loved the calm and encouraging way in which she worked with people; a person-centred approach, before such things were popular in the rehab world. She could bring out the pain that had been buried for many years and hold the patient whilst they shared it. I was always very inspired by her.

The other female counsellor who I loved was a Scottish lady called Sharma, who, although she had excellent boundaries, was always empathic and understanding with a wicked sense of humour. Many years later I tried to tempt her away to join me in a new venture I was developing in Gloucestershire, but she had too many children, and family commitments in Somerset, to move at that time. This was a sad loss for Stepps.

Broadway remains an effective and popular treatment facility, despite some financial difficulties in recent years, and I will always hold it close to my heart, along with the many friends I made there over the years. Whenever I return for a visit and walk through the front doors, I can still feel the safety and healing energy which I felt in 1996. It is a very special place for me and many other people.

Neil

I enjoy life when things are happening. I don't care if it's good things or bad things. That means you're alive.
—Joan Rivers

Whilst working hard in Broadway Lodge one day a new admission was introduced to my therapy group, by my counsellor. He was a strange looking character, wearing Rupert the Bear style trousers, and he made me feel edgy for a reason I could not identify. He opened the group-therapy session by introducing himself as Neil, stating that he had stopped drinking a few years back but was now having problems with cannabis and sex addiction. The rest of the group then individually shared a little about themselves until it was my turn. By this time my body was beginning to shake with anxiety, and I looked at him and said, "My name is Mike and I think that you're a paedophile!" The words were out of my mouth before I had time to process them fully.

He looked devastated and the counsellor raised his voice and said, "Mike! Outside now!" I walked out of the door indignantly, staring at Neil, fully confident that I was right. In the reception area the counsellor stared at me and said, "How dare you say something like that for no reason! Why would you say that? I'm disappointed in you!"

"I don't know why I said it!" I protested. "But I think I'm right!"

The counsellor was very flustered and said, "I think this is your stuff, Mike, not his."

"What is that supposed to mean?" I said in disgust. "How is this my stuff?"

He became more uncomfortable and said, "I mean, you may have some trauma and you may be transferring that onto Neil as he reminds you of something."

"That's rubbish," I said, "I'm telling you he's a paedophile!"

My relationship with Neil was very suspicious and mistrustful on my part and, whenever an opportunity arose in group therapy, I would challenge him brutally as I felt that he was extremely inauthentic in his engagement. Due to the culture in rehabs at that time, often when two people did not get on, they would be put together in the same shared bedroom to bring it to the surface, and often this worked and their issues could be resolved. However, when they did this to me in secondary care, and the only thing separating him from me was a bedside table between our beds, I felt extremely angry. As he was supposedly being treated for sex addiction I wanted to know what his definition of relapse would be and it turned out to be masturbation. So if he was caught 'knocking one out' he should, rightly, be thrown out just as anyone who had had a drink would be. A few days later I woke up in the middle of the night and could hear an uncomfortable noise in the darkness emanating from his bed area. I listened for a few seconds to make sure and, matter-of-factly said, "If you're doing what I think you're doing, I hope you're going to own it in group this morning and then leave." I could sense his shock and embarrassment and heard him jump up and head for the bathroom. "It's not a relapse, Mike, because I didn't climax!" he said as he headed to the door. I was ready for him and said, "Does that mean it's ok for me to walk about all day with a mouth full of vodka provided I don't swallow it? You're talking bollocks and it's time to go!" I said smugly.

As group therapy opened and the counsellor said, "Does anyone want group time?" I stared intimidatingly across the circle at Neil. There was a short silence before he asked for group time and tried to spin it back on me. "Mike feels that I should take group time because of something he thinks he heard in the room last night."

I felt my anger build to a fever pitch and responded before he had even stopped speaking, "Don't even think about trying to push responsibility for this onto me. I know what I heard and you admitted it at the time, so don't sit there and lie! I have a feeling that you've lied about everything since you got here, and until now you've gotten away with it, but your number is up!" The group became unsettled with the allegations and denials, everything was falling into chaos.

The counsellor managed to calm things down and said, "Obviously Neil, I have to take this seriously and discuss the implications with the team, but is there anything that you would like to say to the group before I do?" Again, there was a short silence and I expected him to come back with a new defence however he didn't. He admitted that what I heard was him masturbating, which again brought chaos to the group as the people who had defended him became angry as well.

He then said, "I am here because I have committed sexual acts against children in the past."

"I fuckin' knew it!" I balled across the circle. "I was told it was my stuff and it was fuckin' you all the time, you cunt!" My rage was palpable, and my eyes filled with tears.

The counsellor called the group to order, and Neil said, "Can I finish?" The energy in the circle rose and no one could sit still.

"I have not offended for a long time," he continued, "and I came in here to see if I could work a programme around it but it's very difficult to do that when I can't admit why I'm here! I'm not going to apologise for trying to change my behaviour, but I want to apologise to Mike as he knew right away and has been made to feel like there was something wrong with him." He looked across the floor to me and said, "I'm sorry. I wish I had been able to tell you but, as you can see today, this would have happened." He then looked at the counsellor and said, "You don't need to speak with the team, I will leave as soon as we finish here." In that moment, his humility, his honesty and his empathy for how he had made me feel made my anger begin to dissolve, I felt like my body was beginning to settle down and stop shaking.

As he packed his bags and cleared out of my room, I said to him, "Thank you for finally getting honest and I hope you find some help somewhere else." Then I went downstairs to wait until he left the building. It took me a long time to process and release the anger and stress which the whole situation had caused me, and I also had a serious conversation with the doctor who had agreed to bring him in as there were often children and families visiting. Although it took a little while before I felt safe again, I had learnt the lesson; trust my gut. Even when I was in active addiction, I knew when to leave a situation or who to trust. The only times I was put in danger was when I didn't listen to my instincts.

A Review of My Work-Life

The Royal Scottish National Hospital was a massive site, spread over two separate areas and holding over one-thousand-two-hundred patients. It was made up of individual villas within their own small plots of land, so at the outset of its inception back in the early twentieth century, it was quite forward thinking. Many of the hospitals at that time were huge three or four storey buildings in a central position with most departments housed within the same block. The villas gave some independence to each ward and gave patients a certain level of ownership around their long-term homes. Within the patient population they had their nicknames for each villa and created a hierarchy where they would sarcastically label each other shouting, 'Shut it, Villa-Four boy!' or 'Any more of that and you'll end up in Villa-Five!' On the Old Denny Road end there was the adult hospital which included impressive grounds, a working farm and a variety of architectural designs which included Larbert House, a very grand mansion set slightly outside of the main site.

Close by on the Bellsdyke Road, stood the juvenile hospital which initially held a lot of children and younger patients but which also housed older males and females, plus a couple of geriatric wards. At the very back of the juvenile hospital stood The Pavilions; four children's wards later named Lewis, Tiree, Harris and Jura, after the Scottish Islands. This is where my career started in the long, hot summer of 1976, as a volunteer with Brian McPeake in Lewis ward.

We had decided to give it a try and see how we felt, after we met Ingrid, whilst playing Truant earlier in the year. She suggested, rather than being bored through the summer, we should volunteer and, if we liked it, apply for jobs. On the first day we arrived we met the Senior Nursing Officer Jimmy Taylor who gave us a very brief interview and had us escorted, to Lewis villa, to meet Sister McGowan. She was quite a strict, scary woman, and when she walked into a room, as was the culture of that time, everyone stood up out of respect. Although strict, she invariably had a smile breaking through at the corners of her mouth, and had a very dry sense of humour. She later married Jimmy McKnight, a charge nurse from the adult hospital who was one of the funniest people I have ever worked with. Again his humour was very dry and drole, but hysterically funny. One of the best assessments I ever got was from him, after finishing my placement in Villa-Three or 'Carron', which was one of four villas with sixty beds, for adult males with a range of dependencies. There was also a fifth villa with slightly less beds but with, higher risk, more challenging patients. The infamous Villa-Five was like a semi-secure unit; on-site, where patients who lost control of their behaviours, or who were deemed to be a risk to the public could be contained instead of sending them to Carstairs which was a high-security, special hospital.

The Pavilions were built in the early '60s and were quite modern, glass fronted in their design, with balconies where beds could be brought out in the summer in the high dependency wards Harris and Jura. The interiors were brightly painted with Disney murals, on one wall of each lounge, or parlour as they were known. Lewis held about twenty-five children with varying diagnoses living in there full-time.

Nowadays none of them would ever be admitted to a long stay hospital but the one thing back then was often for paediatricians to advise parents to 'forget this child and go try for another'. I was later to witness this as a student nurse when I sat in on a Paediatric clinic in Falkirk Royal. A young couple who had a child with Down's syndrome were looking for support and guidance in how to best manage their child were told not to waste their time as the child would never get better. Even at that time and as a naïve student I couldn't accept this uncaring and cruel attitude and would often follow parents, back out of the clinic, and say, "Don't listen to all that negativity, nobody knows how your child is going to develop. Do what is best for you as a family." I could never have said that in front of a consultant or my nursing career would have come to a sticky end!

At the end of our first day in Lewis, Brian looked shell-shocked and grey. "I loved it!" I said as we walked to the hospital gates, "what about you?"

"Michael, I hated it," he said, "And I can't come back here." I was taken aback by his response and then realised it may be because he had the most wonderful sister with Down's syndrome called Janey. Everyone in Denny knew her and she was a loving, affectionate and very funny young lady. Brian seemed to me to be struggling with the inequality and unfairness of hospital life which he had seen that day and compared to the full and happy life which Janey enjoyed outside. Our first day was a Friday so I only had the weekend to talk-him-round as I didn't want to be there on my own. I knew I had a hard task ahead of me, so at every opportunity I brought up Lewis and some of the things we had seen and eventually he shouted, "Awright Michael, I'll go back!" I was delighted and looked forward to going back.

Very soon we were a part of the team and got to know all of

the staff very well. One of my favourite people in Lewis was Jean Wilson who also lived in Denny. She was married with a teenage family and worked full time as a nursing assistant in Lewis. She was honest and hard-working, but most of all, we made each other laugh. Whenever I was on shift with her you could hear us laughing all over the ward. She would sometimes fall forward when we were making beds shouting, "Oh Michael, stop, I'm gonna pee myself!" which made me carry on even more. Occasionally Sister McGowan would approach and say, "The laughing hyenas are at it again!" then walk away.

Brian and I knew nothing of protocols, so at the end of every single voluntary shift, as we made our way out of the hospital, we would go to the senior nursing officer's room, knock and open the door and, no matter what was happening in that room, loudly say, "Any jobs yet?"

He was a very pleasant man and would simply say, "Nothing yet boys."

Then we would say, "Thanks." And close the door. After about three months he finally said yes. He gave us a Brown A4 envelope each, which contained application forms for nursing assistants positions.

We were so excited at the time to have the opportunity to get a job as the unemployment situation was bad and we were lucky to be getting this opportunity.

Our friend Pat had started in an apprentice welder position, which was hard work and paid very little, so we felt like we had won the lottery. Soon after we had our first ever interviews and were both offered positions. I was lucky enough to be placed back in Lewis, and Brian was placed in Harris which housed some very disabled and vulnerable children who required round the clock nursing care. I can still remember reading my contract of Whitley terms and conditions and which had an annual salary of around £2000 gross. It worked out that on my early shift week I had £28.00 take home pay and on my late shift week I had £29.00. It seems very little in comparison to today's salaries, but in comparison to my friends who were doing apprenticeships, it was a good pay.

I loved the kids in Lewis. They were a mixed bunch of males and females aged between ten and sixteen, with a range of challenging behaviours, so there wasn't a lot of free-time to sit around. You were always chasing someone who had run away, or were stopping kids from biting each other, or escorting them to the hospital school, or to physio appointments, or horse-riding lessons at a local RDA. It was also very rewarding because many of the kids, despite their difficulties, were very loving and affectionate so we got plenty of cuddles. The downside was that many of them had not been toilet trained so were doubly incontinent, therefore a lot of time was spent 'toileting' the kids. There was also a cutting edge behaviour modification team who would supervise new toilet training, dressing and feeding programmes based on rewarding good behaviours. You always knew when they were in the building as you could hear a chorus of "Good boy, Benjy!" as the sound of trickling pee came from the potty or an arm was successfully placed through a sleeve. We also regularly had student nurses from our own hospital as well as from neighbouring hospitals, working at Lewis on eight week paediatric placements. This was a great experience; to meet students who lived and worked in Glasgow and to hear all of their experiences.

After about two months in my new position, Sister McGowan resigned and moved to England and we were then managed by Sister Hannah who later became a very good friend of mine. Eventually she left, to take up a teaching position, and the decision was made to temporarily close Lewis and I was transferred to Iona ward until a replacement could be found. Iona was an older style of building from the original hospital, with an extension built in. It held a different group of children, some of whom were more able to cognitively engage, but some whom were also a real handful. I remember feeling anxious moving to a new ward with different staff, as I was settled and felt safe in Lewis. It was a fantastic experience though and I met a whole new team of characters to further broaden my horizons. There were a couple of older ladies who had been working in the hospital for many years and whose personalities were as wild as the younger staff. One of these was Nurse McAteer, who was an enrolled nurse and could have me rolling around laughing with just a few words. She did not suffer fools at all, and could cut you dead in your tracks if you did something to upset her, but when she liked you she made the days happier. Another member of the team was an older lady called Kate Comrie who seldom laughed out loud but who was as funny a woman as I've ever met. She would simply make dry, obvious statements in a given moment, which would diffuse any other energy and bring the roof in.

The ward Sister was Anne Hotchkiss, who I admired and got on well with. I was to work with her again in the adult hospital when I was qualified. She was fond of a little drink, so often on a weekend late shift, once everyone was in bed she would pour a whisky in the office and say, "Get that down, you, it's been a hard week." And we would throw it down in one.

Alcohol was a common remedy for the staff. Although technically a sacking offence senior managers knew that it only happened at parties, outings and occasionally after the patients were asleep, so they didn't make a big deal of it. Only when parties got out of hand in ways such as setting off fire alarms and wasting the extinguishers was action taken which made everyone more cautious again, for a while. This would sometimes happen when students from other hospitals were leaving and their behaviour would escalate until people found themselves being thrown into cold baths of water. The students had already completed their training assessments, and since they were leaving anyway they didn't care what they did. The '70s were a wilder time, and many of those behaviours would never be acceptable today, thank God. I made some good friends amongst the Iona staff, including Liz Fisher who went on to marry my friend Pat.

I enjoyed my time in Iona but, after about three months Lesley Slade was appointed the role of Sister at Lewis and the building reopened. I was so happy to be back in the pavilions, it felt like coming home although it wasn't quite the same as it had been previously, it felt like there was a bit of resistance to the new Sister by the older staff as they had heard rumours about her sexuality. I found her to be very motivated and energetic, as she always wanted the kids to be doing things, whereas the staff liked their cigarette and tea-breaks which were lessened because of her activities programmes. It was at this point that I applied and was accepted into a student nurse position and, in September 1978, I said goodbye to all of my safety and friendships in Lewis and headed further down the road to the School of Nursing at Bellsdyke Hospital. It was a very sad moment for me; leaving my first job, but I knew it was the right thing to do and that if I didn't, I could end up as institutionalised as some of the unhappy and negative staff whom I had worked with over the last two years.

Nurse Training

My three-year training course started with an eight week educational block in the school of nursing which was situated in 'The Huts' at Bellsdyke Hospital. The Huts were old and not really fit for purpose, but they were my home for all of my education over the first two years before we moved to newer buildings in Callender Park, Falkirk. Bellsdyke was a large mental health hospital with a similar villa system as the RSNH. There were around thirty students in my class, made up of around half RSNH and half Bellsdyke students. The first few days were interesting with everyone finding their preferred groups and forming friendships. I already knew a few people, so it wasn't so difficult, although I made some new friends including Patricia Sobasz, whom I sat next to every day on the long journey taken by the Dunipace bus, and Susan Cairney from Grangemouth both of whom laughed all day long. They were great to be around and if I needed cheering up I would just sit down with them for a few minutes. The teaching team was led by John Baxter who we nicknamed 'Burton's Dummy' as he was always immaculately dressed in a three-piece suit and looked smart. He was supported by Margaret Hannah, Jim Ritchie, Anna Kerr, Ronnie Neil and Charlie McLaughlin. Learning from them could be very tedious as they weren't all trained teachers so they often spoke in monotonous voices. I swear I lost my interest in Biology because of Ronnie Neil's thick Belfast accent and slow delivery when reading directly from Ross and Wilsons; which was the standard anatomy and physiology textbook at the time. I remember nodding off when he took an afternoon session because he generally just read a chapter out loud and that was it. Some of the others made a bit more of an effort to liven up their sessions by doing interactive role plays and first aid lessons, but none of it was life-changing and more often than not, like high school, I spent most of my time making others laugh.

The second year was more exciting as we were sent on placements to general hospitals to cover medical and surgical nursing, midwifery and then to district nursing and health visiting placements. I loved Stirling Royal Infirmary and learned so much in my placements. Working at Medical Ward One was a very exciting experience, working with adults who'd had heart failure, strokes etc. It was my first ever experience of a cardiac arrest setting off the alarm and getting the trolley and bed ready for the defibrillator to shock someone back to life or, on some occasions, not. You could feel your adrenaline rush in that moment as you tried to save a life, and the joy if it was successful was immense, just as the sadness and disappointment was painful if it wasn't. I have seldom worked in a team that was so unified as Ward One and I was sad to leave. I was then placed in Ward Six with its infamous Ward Sister; a skilled nurse, but a monster to work with, shouting and shaming her staff at every turn, in order she believed, to get the best out of them.

She always seemed to single me out and call, "Nurse Delaney!" across the ward, in the knowledge that I didn't like the title and always responded with, "Michael, please." However she would not deviate from the Florence Nightingale bedside manual and ruled the roost with a fist of iron.

I remember my uncle being admitted for a haemorrhoid operation. He was my dad's brother and we were close, so when the Sister said to me, "Nurse Delaney, please prep the lower body and genital area of bed six for surgery!"

I immediately protested and said, "Sister, he is my uncle, and I don't want to do such an intimate procedure; it would be extremely embarrassing for both of us."

She looked at me with a cruel spark in her eye and said, "You will do what you're told, Nurse Delaney, or your assessment from me will reflect that failure!"

"Sister, I'm sure that what you're asking me to do is unethical and I don't want to do it!" I firmly replied.

But she clearly wasn't used to being challenged and became very angry. "Are you refusing an instruction? Do you want your career to end here and now?" she screamed into my face, so I turned on my heel like an angry child and stormed off to get my shaving-trolley ready, feeling so much rage that I was being forced into doing something so personal on a family member.

I explained to my uncle before I started and he said, "Don't worry, Michael, I won't say anything if you don't" which made me laugh.

On another occasion another relative who happened to be a local priest came in for the very same operation and, again, she said, "Nurse Delaney, prep the Father in bed three for a haemorrhoidectomy!"

"Please, Sister," I replied, "He is my cousin and will be very embarrassed if he has to have his lower regions shaved by me!" The same 'Terminator look' came into her eyes and I knew arguing was futile; I would have to exact my revenge in some other way before I left. I proceeded to pull the screens and to shave a serving priest's nether regions, and I knew that he was dying of embarrassment. I was later sent to supervise his first bowel movement post-op so I arrived behind the screens with my commode, in full mask and gown and said, "Father, I'll leave you for a few minutes to give you some privacy then I'll come back and check everything's ok."

As humbly as always he said, "Thank you, Michael. God bless you."

I was doing something to kill time at the other end of the ward when I suddenly realised that I hadn't left him toilet roll with the commode. I rushed to the sluice-room and grabbed a toilet roll for him and discreetly went back behind his screens. "So sorry, Father, I forgot to give you toilet roll," I whispered but as I looked at the commode it was full of newspaper and I realised that he had wiped his bottom with The Catholic Universe! I was mortified and wanted to laugh out loud but had to keep my composure because he would have been so embarrassed.

After four weeks of torture, it was my last day and I was due my assessment, which was an ongoing format that was given back to a student after each placement, so once it was written it couldn't be changed. My revenge was set. I was supposed to finish at two p.m. and by one forty-five she still hadn't called me to her office. She had done the others from my group, but not me, so I was beginning to get angry. At two p.m. she called me in, and despite her attempts to bully and intimidate me I knew I had done well as everyone else from the staff team and the patients had said so.

She proceeded to go through my assessment, slowly and deliberately as she knew I would miss my bus; however I have to say that her assessment was honest and fair. After about forty-five minutes she asked me to sign if I agreed, which I did, then she placed it in an A4 envelope and handed it to me. Now, it couldn't be changed, no matter what. I stood up to leave her office and said, "Sister, can I say something?"

"Yes," she replied, expecting a compliment because she had given me a good assessment.

I looked her straight in her steely eyes and said, "You're a nasty, vindictive old cunt!" and watched her face turn scarlet with rage in a millisecond. She drew in breath to call me back, but I quickly said, "No witnesses!" Then slammed her office door behind me. I then began an adrenalin-fuelled run through the corridors, knowing that she was somewhere behind me trying to catch up and get the assessment back! I have always hated bullies and felt that it was an injustice if they got away with it. I sat on the Denny bus on my way home with my assessment intact and a knowing smile on my face.

The only time I returned to work in Stirling Royal was a short spell in the maternity unit as part of my midwifery placement, but I soon asked if I could transfer to Falkirk as it was such a depressing environment. I used to despair at the fact that so many older ward sisters had come into nursing to help people but were actually horrible bullies to everyone. I often had similar thoughts about some of the nuns I had come across. There was a particular sister in the maternity ward who was such a character; unhappy, angry, shaming and cruel. When patients left with their babies they would hand in chocolates, sweets and biscuits for the nurses which she would take into her office, open and then eat the ones she liked! Eventually, the half-eaten carcasses of the boxes would be left in the kitchen for the staff. She hated me on sight, because people liked me, especially the patients. It was the first year that male midwives had been trained in Scotland and she was not happy about it; men coming into her ward and doing stuff that only women were supposed to know about. She was obsessive about tidiness and polished floors, so I spent my time deliberately planting mess, just so that I could hear her roar,

"Who's left this mess here?" all over the ward.

I would say to the patients, who were terrified of her, "Watch this" as I would change the position of screens and curtains so that they were uneven, and pull back and ruffle a couple of bedspreads on empty beds. She would soon appear and shout, "Who's been in this ward? Who pulled these curtains?" And I would see the women slide down under their covers to hide their laughter, "Michael, you're gonna burst my stitches making me laugh!" was a regular cry from beneath the covers!

That was my favourite game, it was the funniest thing. One day I was wearing a certain pair of black shoes which I noticed occasionally left a dark scuff mark on her light coloured, highly polished floors. She appeared from her office at one point and called out, "Who's putting black marks on my floors?" I had already warned the women and I could see them pretending to read or sleep in order to avoid eye contact. From then on, every time she left the ward for a break, or a meeting, or lunch I used to make the women scream, tap-dancing in the middle of the ward, leaving about a square-metre of polished lino looking like a nursery school had visited armed with black crayons and drawn all over the floor.

I would look busy on her return to the ward. I would hear her roar at the women and any staff who were on the floor, "Who's doing this to my floors? Tell me!"

"I was just dozing, Sister, I didn't see anyone" would be the general response. "Someone must have seen!" she would scream. "I'll find out who it is, and woe betide them when I'm done with them!" she would bellow before locking herself in the office with the latest supply of chocolates.

I much preferred the maternity unit at Falkirk Royal, where I was properly taught, and included in the ward team. I did my full placement and case studies in ante-natal, post-natal and labour wards and I loved the whole experience. Being present and assisting in the delivery of a baby remains high on my 'beautiful experiences of my life' list. There is something so very powerful about new life arriving onto our planet and being the first person to hold that life in your hands, checking that all the vital signs are there. But as powerful as it is when something goes wrong, it is the nurse's responsibility to have the baby be given suction or be rushed to the ICU for incubation. I was very lucky, to be able to do my whole case-study about the same person as my placements fell in the right order. I met my patient in ante-natal, and worked with her prior to her water breaking and labour commencing. I was then on-duty when this happened, so was allowed to be with her in the delivery suite. She was quite a large lady and the teaching at that time said that larger women often have smaller babies so, as the labour progressed, I was expecting this small arrival. I will never forget when the head appeared, very large and covered in thick black hair. There was a short period of controlled breathing before the whole body arrived. She looked like a two-year-old, and I couldn't believe a woman could bear such pain, such discomfort and produce such a beautiful being. The midwife cleared the airways and the baby let out a scream, so we headed over to the scales. "Thirteen pounds, fourteen ounces," the midwife said loudly, and I looked at the mother with my mouth hanging open.

"Are you kidding me?" she said as she smiled at me.

"She'll be able to go home in a baby walker!" I said and we started to laugh.

The other side of my year of placements in Stirling and Falkirk was the social life. Back then, there was no support in the form of clinical supervision, or debriefing, or just plain mentorship so the social life of a nurse was very important. It gave a safety valve for letting off steam after a busy or, as often happened, traumatic day. General nurses and midwives are always at the sharp end of healthcare, where things don't always go to plan and patients are lost despite the efforts made by the staff. Even after years of experience, this doesn't get easier, and often the experienced nurses on a shift will take on the difficult tasks; like telling relatives about a death, as they want to protect the younger nurses.

Death is as important a journey as birth, and also needs to be managed with dignity, understanding and respect. I witnessed several deaths during my placements and also spent time in the theatre watching surgeries and, on one occasion, watching a post-mortem. I wouldn't label that as a pleasant experience, but it was absolutely fascinating to watch a pathologist work out how someone had died. This is the reason that shows such as CSI and Silent Witness are so popular as we gain insights into the information which our body holds.

At both Stirling and Falkirk, but equally at the Larbert Hospitals, my social life was often frenetic and intense. I found that, the challenge of trying to be a mature professional was often at odds with the expected behaviour and social life of a teenager. We weren't doing the manual labour of say, a factory or shop worker, but I always envied the fact that they could leave work at five p.m. and not think about it until the following day, whereas we were dealing with human relationships and all their complexities. Sometimes it was very difficult to balance between the two, especially when you have developed a relationship with someone who suddenly passes, and you are expected not to be attached or emotional. That is when the drink at the pub becomes the lock-in, the reason for going to parties, which could then easily become something else, with arguments and fights, or interestingly, casual sex. Nobody ever taught us about how to manage feelings or how to come down after a traumatic shift at work. We were expected to be professional without giving us the underpinning knowledge of how to do that, so often we just had to pretend or act as if we were OK. The culture at the time was also not conducive to sharing feelings. Men had to be men and women had to be women. If you cried or felt upset, you were weak and ineffective. If you were detached and unaffected by anything you were professional and trustworthy. My need to share and process my daily experiences with others had been pre-empted by the many years I had spent heading to the pub. At the end of every shift and meeting my friendship groups: other nurses who knew how I felt and were doing the same as me in order to get through it. My tribe. My friends. My support. When I became qualified in Larbert this included my childhood friends Pat and Brian, but also my work colleagues and friends such as Val and Karen who supported and partied with me for years!

After a number of other jobs, which are highlighted in other chapters, in 1987 I decided to return to nursing as I was fed-up with the service industry and putting up with rude customers. I was living in Stratford with Peter, so I initially applied for a school-nurse position at Whitefield School which was a highly regarded special-school for young people with learning disabilities. I was interviewed by a panel led by a very nice lady called Doris, who was a senior nurse manager based at Thorpe Coombe Hospital in Walthamstow. After the interview she asked me to stay behind and have a chat with her, so I returned to the waiting room and took a seat. She came out and signalled for me to come with her into a small office and we sat at a table, "Mike," she said, "The reason I want to talk to you is that you are so experienced and skilled in what you do that I don't think Whitefield would be a good fit for you. You would get bored very quickly as, really, you're over-qualified for this position."

Eager to get the job I said, "Oh, but I really like the look of the school and the work you are doing here, so it is something that I am really interested in." But she wasn't for moving.

"I have an idea," she said.

"There is a lady called Geraldine who is a service manager based in Leytonstone and she is looking for CPNs (Community Psychiatric Nurses) to join her team. The hospital is planned for closure and all the services will become community based so they are expanding. I'll give her a call and she will call you for interview." Although disappointed, I was intrigued by this development so agreed and we shook hands on it.

Within a couple of days, a brown envelope came through the door inviting me for an interview, so I put my suit on again and headed to Leytonstone House, a small hospital site by the Green Man roundabout. I was invited upstairs and shown into Geraldine Swain's office. She was a very pleasant and down to earth lady with shoulder-length brown hair and dressed in a long flowing dress and Birkenstock sandals. She had a tray of tea brought in and then said, "Mike, Doris called me because she was very impressed by you and felt that your talents would not have been right for the school position. Is there any reason why you don't want to go back into a mainstream nursing role?"

"That's a long story," I replied with a smile, "I guess I just got fed-up with the hamster-wheel; the stress and the dramas of hospital work. Whitefield just felt like it was something different." She then proceeded to tell me about the reprovision plans and how their community nursing services would be expanding. She sold the service well and assured me that I would have a wide variety of experiences as a CPN and that it would be very different from hospital work. After a short time discussing she asked, "How would you feel about joining us?"

In a dour tone I said, "OK, I'll give it a bash." And the deal was done. She then took me down to the Portakabin where the team were based and introduced me firstly to Jacques the senior nurse, then to Ben and Helen who were both CPNs sitting at desks in the shared office. They made me a coffee and we sat chatting for a while before Geraldine said that she had to go and wished me well. Everyone then relaxed and it felt really comfortable. Jacques and Ben were both from Mauritius and had worked in the NHS for a long time. Helen was from Upminster in Essex and had a young son. As I sat at the empty desk which would become mine, I listened and began to believe that this could be a good idea. They seemed really nice and very contented in their roles and, when I found out what my salary would be, I was very happy to join them.

My four years in that position were generally very happy and I developed strong friendships with everyone in the team which did expand, as promised. Eventually we were joined by Moira, who sadly passed away suddenly after a couple of years in the position, and Phil McCoy whom I was already friends with. We all got on very well and there was a lot of laughter in that office.

Over that time, I also became very close friends with Jacques and his wife Iris who had two young children, Philo and Michael and lived in Leytonstone. At one point when I could not find accommodation, they allowed me to stay with them for a few weeks whilst I got myself sorted out. I spent many evenings with them, drinking and dancing and singing the nights away. Although I loved them dearly, I became aware that my relationship with them was not helping my increasing dependence on alcohol and drugs. Often when I stayed over Jacques and I would be up very late drinking rum or vodka, then, in the morning we would go out to the local pub and start drinking pints. Often, I would be sick but would carry on regardless. Many times, I would end up vomiting into the gutter and all I could hear was Jacques hysterical laughter in the background but both him and Iris were very generous and loyal friends!

Meeting 'Grace' Kelly

A good laugh overcomes more difficulties and dissipates more dark clouds than any other one thing.
—Laura Ingalls Wilder

After working in a restaurant named Oliver Twist, for some time, I was approached by a guy called Brian who ran a large gay pub in Poplar called The George IV. Him and his staff, including the infamous Laurie Lush and Blanche Dubois, had eaten at the restaurant several times and seemed to enjoy the food.

He was at the bar paying me what was owed by his table and, as he handed me his credit card he said, "Do you work Sundays, Mike?"

"No, Brian, I have Sundays off," I replied as I dragged the credit card machine from left to right and handed him the flimsy receipt to sign.

"How do you fancy running a Sunday lunch at the George? You can bring in your own waiters, we can lay the whole pub up as restaurant tables that customers book and we will have live cabaret on the stage all afternoon!" he said temptingly. "I'll pay you £75 cash!" Now that was what I wanted to hear, as that was a good rate in 1985, and I knew that tips would then take that to well over £100.

"You've got a deal, Brian. When do you want to start?" I said enthusiastically.

"Well, I need to do some ordering, and a little bit of

advertising, so how about two weeks? In the meantime can you come over and let me know what you need for the front of the house? I've got a great chef called Tilly who will do a great traditional lunch but I don't have anyone who knows how to work a floor like you so I can also give you £100 to pay two waiters to support you," he said in a delighted tone as he shook my hand.

"I'll pop in tomorrow and have a chat," I said as their taxis arrived and they left.

"What was all that whispering about?" said Jimmy as he drunkenly locked the front door of the restaurant then perched himself opposite me on a bar-stool. "Don't lie to your mother!" he said, before falling over laughing at his own joke.

"You don't pay me enough, Jimmy!" I replied. "So he's offered me a Sunday gig which pays very well. Any objections?"

"Me? Object? How dare you!" He scowled under waves of a very dirty sounding laugh. In hindsight I would say that Jimmy was probably on the high functioning end of the autistic spectrum, but nobody would have been aware of that in his childhood. During the day he always seemed agitated and rude to people. Emotionally he didn't connect very well at all and was always doing something to keep his mind occupied, but after a few drinks he became this totally different, hysterically funny character. A few drinks made him feel like anyone else, it seemed, to me.

A few months before moving into the Oliver Twist, I was doing casual work for a catering company who had a contract in Kensington Town Hall which was a very grand place to work. I was earning a very good daily rate and was commuting back and forth from South Croydon every day. It was very much 'silver service', which I learned on the job, and they held many large functions on different floors simultaneously. We had a core team of four or five of us and extra, casual staff came in daily. One of these was an out of work actor called Sean, whose claim-to-fame had been his time playing the desk sergeant in Z Cars. He was full of very funny and interesting stories about different people he had met, but I often had to say, "Sean, we have to get these tables laid!" as he couldn't multi-task!

He came in one day and told me that he had been offered a position as head-waiter at a new place in the East End which was just opening, and he asked if I would be interested in coming with him. "Sean, I doubt they will pay anything like I get paid here so I don't see how it would benefit me really," I said as I signalled for him to lay cups as he was talking. "Yes, it's less money, Mike, but it includes accommodation and all meals so you don't have to think about that and even on the money you're making here, you couldn't afford London rents."

He was right and the more I spoke to him, the more I thought it might be worth considering. By the time I had paid rent in Croydon and then train fares, it may be worth considering exchanging money for stability. He suggested that I do a trial shift the following week, and see how I felt, which sounded like a good idea. On the following Saturday afternoon, I arrived for my trial night and overnight stay. As I walked out of Aldgate East Stations underpass onto Leman Street, I thought, 'Oh fuck, this is a bit rough.' It looked very run-down, but there was also a lot of building work going on. Sean had warned me but explained that the Docklands were being redeveloped so it would all gradually be upgraded. At the other end of the road stood the Oliver Twist Restaurant, sitting right next door to The Brown Bear Public House.

I pushed the large green door, walking into the restaurant and found myself facing a small bar area, with dark wood panelling on top of magnolia coloured artexed plasterwork. The carpet was dark green and heavily patterned to hide the stains, and in the corner was a staircase which went down to the main cellar and restaurant area with its low arched ceilings. Although quite dark and dingy, with a slightly damp and musty smell, it had a bit of character and a certain charm. Sean approached the door and gave me a bear hug. "Jimmy, this is Mike, who I was telling you about," he said as this very thin, miserable looking man approached.

"Hello," he said in an awkward way. "You found us OK then? I wish more fucking punters would!" he said in a very dry tone.

"Is business bad then?" I asked in a bid to connect with his spiky attitude.

"Put it this way," he responded. "For the past two nights the only money that's been put into that fucking till was mine!" Sean looked at me and did some kind of signalling with his eyes. He knew I could be mouthy and that I definitely didn't put up with anyone speaking down to me so I thought he must be asking me to hold on and see what would happen.

Jimmy invited me to sit down with him and Sean, and then he called into the kitchen. "Sandwiches for three!" Like a sergeant major, with no politeness or even a please. I looked at Sean again and he shook his head and stared at me. Once more I said nothing. "Sean told me he works with you and that you're very good," Jimmy said in a slightly warmer tone. "I'm looking for a bar manager who knows about different wines and ordering, how and when to serve different drinks and also cashier duties, keeping tabs on all the bills. The staff are very young and inexperienced, so you'll need to keep an eye on them. Sean says you're a bit fiery so I'll keep you away from serving tables if I can!" This broke the ice and made me laugh out loud and so did they, which lifted the atmosphere. As we ate sandwiches and drunk lager we agreed a cash salary, plus tips, and I had Saturday in the daytime and all-day Sunday off. The only room available was in the attic space and was very basic, although I had my own bathroom, but if any of the other staff left, I could move downstairs and get their room. I stayed there for two years, when he sold the building, and then the new owners asked me to stay following a huge refurbishment.

Back in The George, the Sunday lunches really took off, it was packed, sometimes there would even be enough customers to fill The George twice over the course of the day. The licensing laws at the time allowed all day opening on Sundays if food was served, so it was a cash cow as there was nowhere else in the East End doing anything so adventurous. I would go in on a Sunday morning and lay up all the tables in cloths and cutlery, condiments, napkins and table numbers. I would meet with Tilly who would roughly gauge how many portions of each different meat we could serve. Tilly worked in the upstairs kitchen and everything came down via the manually hoisted dumb waiter at the end of the bar. Just before twelve the waiters would arrive and, on this particular day I had employed my friend from home; Maggie who worked in The Roebuck in Belsize Park and would do shifts for me when she got a Sunday off. Like me, she didn't take any nonsense so the punters loved her, and I could always hear the laughter when she was serving tables. There was also a top-class cabaret, of the likes of Lily Savage, to keep the punters laughing.

On this particular day, I was sorting out some chaos at the dumb waiter, over Tilly sending down the wrong meals, when Maggie came up to me. "Michael, there's a guy over there says he's from Denny! I don't know him, but he says he knows me. Goan speak to him and see who he is," she said.

I followed her round the bar to where she was serving and said loudly, "Who's from Denny?"

With a smile, "Me!" said this handsome guy about my age, dressed like a new pin and smelling of Paco Rabanne.

"You look about my age so I should know you," I said as I looked at him curiously. "What's yer name?" I asked.

"Michael Kelly," he replied. "What's yours?"

"Michael Delaney," I said, "but I don't seem to remember you."

"Delaney?" he said, "did you live in Gorrie Street?"

"Yeah, we did," I replied, still not recognising him.

He stood up beside me and said, "I left Denny when I was fifteen 'cos my parents split up and we moved down to Norfolk." I was still lost as to who he may be as the only Michael Kelly I could think of was in my class at St Pat's and lived in Perth.

He then said, "You probably saw me in a ladies blue, fitted duffle-coat, bumping a silver cross pram full of washing down to the launderette at weekends!" The minute he painted that picture I knew who he was and I remembered speaking to him on different occasions and smoking with him behind the bike sheds.

"Oh my God, Michael, I remember you!" I bellowed at the top of my lungs.

"Did you wear glessies?" he asked me with a hint of recognition in his eyes.

"Aye! I worked in Petale's ice cream van, and you bought single cigarettes!" The two of us fell about laughing, and after my food service was over, I sat with him and his friends. We were struggling to speak we were laughing so much, talking about different people we knew and how difficult it was to be gay in

Denny. "I blame the fitted duffle coat!" he screamed as he told stories of getting into fights when people called him names.

"I remember wondering about you!" he said knowingly. "Can you imagine if we had been able to talk to each other? Maybe our lives would have been different." How true those words were. He lived only a few hundred yards from me, but we never connected on a meaningful level. I would probably have denied it if he had asked me if I was gay. How sad that such a potentially life-changing friendship, for both of us, was not possible. We drunk and laughed into the night and he came back and stayed in the restaurant where we continued to talk all night. From then on, we were like long lost brothers. We understood each other so well and we also respected each other's ability to survive a difficult upbringing and have the strength to continue to survive a culture which was hostile to gays. We turned everything possible into a joke and joined forces when anyone or anything posed a threat to the other. We had each other's backs. About a year after our first meeting, we met on a Saturday afternoon after he phoned the restaurant to check I was there. He arrived and said, "Shall we go next door to The Brown Bear for a drink? I have some news for you." He looked a bit pale and shocked, so I asked if he was OK. "I need a drink, before I start talking about it," he replied in a very solemn tone. I was getting worried.

We got two pints of lager from the landlady May and sat down at a corner table. "What's going on Michael?" I asked, beginning to really worry about him. For the first time since I had met him in The George, I saw his eyes fill with tears.

"I've got HTLV-3," he said. There was silence as he started to shake uncontrollably, and silent tears ran down his face.

"Oh my God, Michael," I said to him as I felt my own tears

begin to fall. This was 1985 in London, and at that point there was no treatment to speak of, and the only prognosis was death. We were in the corner of a pool room where heavy drinking Irishmen were drinking and farting, so I couldn't even hug him.

He saw the irony in the situation. "Do you think I should tell them and see if they can help?" he said, before bursting into hysterical laughter, followed by me. The emotional release was happening but just not in the right way!

After the hysteria died down, I asked, "What are you gonna do then?"

"I've got an appointment at Chelsea and Westminster, next week to look at treatment options," he said. "But you know as well as I do, there's nothing out there." I looked at him sitting there, twenty six years old, handsome, not a bad person in any way; in fact an example of strength and resilience and now he had to try and manage this new and deadly diagnosis. I had known about AIDS since before I moved to England, because I was a nurse and it was in the professional journals, long before it was in the media and I had already known several people who had suddenly just vanished – but now it was on my doorstep and was killing my closest friend.

"Whatever happens, Michael," I said as I looked into his eyes, "whatever happens, I'm here for you."

"Thanks, Son," he said quietly, followed by, "let's get pished!"

In the coming months Michael did what he did best. He went into denial and just carried on with his life, although he did always attend hospital appointments and GP reviews, his health at that point was very good so he almost began to doubt the diagnosis. It wasn't until doctors started explaining his T cell count and viral load that he fully accepted that he was ill, but he still did not allow it to affect his life, and we continued to party for several years before his health began to deteriorate. We were complete lunatics and became well known on the East London Scene as 'The two Michaels'. There was also another couple called The Two Michaels who tragically drowned when the Marchioness sunk in the Thames. I remember going into The George a few weeks later with Michael and feeling very struck by the way the pub fell silent when we walked in and the expressions on people's faces. "What the fuck's going on here?" I said to Michael as we got to the bar.

"I'm fucked if I know, Son, lager for me!" he replied.

At that point a local character called Penny came running up to us both with tears streaming, shouting, "Oh God, I thought you was both dead!" He began to cuddle us both.

"Where did you get that idea?" I asked in puzzlement but by that time a few others had joined us and were also agreeing that they thought it was us.

Suddenly, Ida Street walked in and said, "No, not those Michaels, the English couple."

We both knew them as well and said, "Oh fuck, what a shock." We knew about the Marchioness but not too many details about who was on board.

If I were to sum up my years with Michael, I would say, in all honesty there was never a dull moment, we fed off each-others humour and personality and neither of us wanted to sit at home watching TV.

Over the years we shared flats together three times, usually having to move out because we hadn't paid rent, but even when we lived separately, we saw or spoke to each other every single day. The AIDS crisis only worsened and Thatcher's government did nothing to help, in fact they brought in Clause 28 which made it illegal to discuss homosexuality in schools; thereby alienating and shaming another generation. We gradually lost more and more friends, every day until it felt like we were trapped in The Twilight Zone. Every time we went out, someone else had gone, and another funeral was booked usually with only friends in attendance because a lot of families had disowned or rejected their gay sons. I remember once going to three funerals on the same day and not being shocked by that. Three young men, with their whole lives ahead of them, cut down, dead and buried without a mention. There was another day that Michael picked me up with Laurie Lush, and we rushed late to our friend George's funeral in Wanstead. We parked the car and ran to the graveside, where the mourners were all gathered, and Michael said, "Thank God, we've made it."

In time to hear the clergyman say, "We celebrate the life of Margaret…" We all looked at each other and burst out laughing with the shock as we stepped-back from the graveside and returned to the car to discover it was Wanstead crematorium and not the cemetery.

By 1990, I felt traumatised and exhausted. The AIDS crisis was taking its toll and, most days I felt lost and confused. I was drinking and doing drugs in the extreme and had debts coming out of my ears; although I had always been careful, I was very frightened of getting HIV, but I also felt a sense of guilt because I hadn't.

It was years later, after Michael's death, that I would understand and appreciate the absolute trauma and shame which I experienced in the 1980s. People may have looked-on and assumed that we were all having a great time, but it was the only way we could survive. When AIDS became a national talking point, and the government were posting frightening leaflets through everyone's doors, the backlash against the gay community was immediate and harsh. The tabloids played a major role in demonising gay men and calling AIDS a 'Gay Plague'. Comedians like Bernard Manning made people laugh by joking about queers dying. The government did nothing to help. Queer-bashing became its own epidemic. Gay men lost their jobs, couldn't get life insurance, were humiliated at every turn, and despite that, stayed strong and focused. I, however, was burned-out. I could not carry on losing everyone without dying from liver failure or a nervous breakdown myself, as I was probably suffering from PTSD. In a misguided, and irrational moment, I decided to leave London and move to the North of England to escape my perpetual routine of death and funerals. I would return five years later, to support Michael through his terminal care, and then would really find out what trauma was.

Jimmy

We understand death only after it has placed its hands on someone we love.
—Anne L. de Stael

As I got to know Jimmy, the owner of the Oliver Twist restaurant I understood him better, and realised that his brusque attitude and disconnectedness were not intentional, but a way of getting what he needed in a given moment without flannel or unnecessary chit-chat, which, unless he was drunk, he clearly struggled with. He would arrive by nine in the morning and join his long-time friend and employee Bob, who ran a small book-keeping and accountancy business from the office. They were nicknamed Mapp and Lucia, as together they would get into silly arguments about nothing, and would have minor fallouts. They had been friends for many years though and this is just how their relationship worked. Bob was a very quick witted and funny old queen, always sending a one-liner across the room. He and his long-term partner ran a boutique together for many years before he died, and I think it was grief which threw him into the clutches of Jimmy. They acted like deadly enemies but were actually very reliant on each other. When they got drunk sitting at the bar some evenings, the secrets and lies would pour out of them. One story which made me laugh loudly was when Jimmy told me that, many years previously, Bob's boutique had run into major financial difficulties and him and his partner decided that a fire would give them enough insurance to clear their feet. On the day that the deed was due to happen, they both left the shop and went for lunch in a nearby restaurant so that the job could be carried out. The story goes that, after the table had been cleared following the main course, one of the waiters came running in from outside screaming, "Sir! Your shop is on fire! It's ablaze!"

There was a moment's silence before Bob replied, "Can I see the dessert menu, please?" This ability to subvert anything with a quick response was admirable in both of them.

After opening in the mornings, Jimmy would come to the bar and say, "Half of lager, please." And I would pour a glass of draft Carlsberg. He would then have maybe four or five before he went home to change in the afternoon. Every evening he would return at five p.m., showered and suited-up, ready for whatever the evening brought. He came into his own in the evenings because he drank heavily and lost all of his daytime agitation. As he walked in the front door, he would smile at me and say, "I think I'll have a G+T to start this evening." He would then have several as he ordered whatever he fancied from the menus, usually a steak with a heavy cream sauce. He always sat at a table in the bar area in the evenings so that he could see the comings and goings of the customers. Just before his main course he would choose whatever wine he fancied from our extensive list, which I would open and serve.

He always had a full bottle, sometimes two, or if he had invited company three or four would be demolished. When he was done with the wine, he would have either a dessert or cheese and biscuits which also meant either port or a sweet wine was served with it. Finally, he would pull up a barstool, sit across from me at the bar, flutter his eyelashes and say, "Darling, could I have a Brandy?" The rest of the night would be hysterical as he could be extremely funny and would quite often fall over. When it was closing time, he would pull on this suede duffle-coat with a large hood which, from behind made him look like Obi-Wan Kenobi from Star Wars. When he finally left, me and the other staff would watch, laughing as he careened all over the road trying to walk in a straight line.

This happened every night, except Sundays when we were closed, and he would eat somewhere else with one of his friends, yet he had no physical problems such as shakes or vomiting, in fact he had a Harley Street doctor who regularly ran blood screens which showed extremely healthy liver and kidney function. I have witnessed him lying unconscious at a party at four o'clock in the morning and then be ready for work at nine a.m. the same morning, bright-eyed and bushy-tailed, and he was around fifty years old at the time. He had a chequered history and was involved with some of the early clubs in London such as The Pink Panther. Back then he knew the high and mighty of the time, and had a wonderful lifestyle which he would yearn for when he was drunk. He had also spent some time in prison, and there were often unmarked cars sitting outside the restaurant. I mentioned it one night and said, "Jimmy, that car has been sitting there for a couple of days, are they watching the restaurant?"

"They're trying to track down the money!" he replied with a smile. He later told me that he became a millionaire by selling pornography through a mail order catalogue, in unmarked brown envelopes.

"But that wasn't illegal, was it?" I asked innocently.

"Well, some of it was a bit hard-core," he said. "But I was jailed because I had run my business for years with a stolen franking machine so I never paid postage!" he let out a high-pitched cackle as he said that and I couldn't stop laughing at the sheer nerve of him!

Two years after he bought the restaurant, a five storey Victorian building for peanuts, he sold it for a huge amount at the time and made a nice profit. It was a nice end to a couple of happy years without responsibility, or pressure, a time when I could really let myself go and not be concerned about professional obligations. I recently visited that building which is now an Indian restaurant on the ground floor and basement, with the three remaining floors being individual apartments valued at over one-million pounds each.

Michael, the Last Days

Do you not know that a man is not dead while his name is still spoken?
—Terry Pratchett

It was early 1995 when I left my home in the North West of England and travelled town to London, I had spoken to Michael on the phone and he was getting close to the end. I promised him five years previously that I would come and help look after him when he was ready, so that he could die at home. My sisters Eileen and Judith, and their partners Chris and Sean, as well as our cousin Steven, and a few others had been doing a grand job of round-the-clock care at his North London flat. When I arrived, the shock of simply seeing him was profound. My dearest friend who was my height and my build was shrivelled up and hardly made a bump in his bedclothes. Cytomegalovirus had spread through his spinal cord and caused blindness. He was skin and bone, around five stone I would imagine, with open bed-sores due to his bony joints sticking through. He was being nursed on ripple beds and wore sheepskin knee and ankle protectors. He was attached to a syringe driver dispensing good quantities of morphine so at least I knew he wasn't in pain. "Hiya, Son," I whispered as I gently leaned over and kissed him.

His eyes slowly opened and he said, "Oh Michael, ye made it. Thanks, Son." He touched my face.

"How are you feeling?" I asked, realising what a stupid

question it was and feeling my emotions bubbling just below the surface.

"Well, I don't think we'll be going out clubbing, son, but I'm OK. Your amazing family have stepped up and really taken care of me, and I'm not always an easy patient!" I sat with him on his bed for a while and took in the enormity of what was about to happen. He was drifting in and out of consciousness, and although very frail, he was also very strong and, intellectually, still as sharp as a tack!

In the sitting room I caught up with my family and got a sense of how he had been, and it transpired that he had been having some trouble with nurses as he tended to be rude and demanding at times. I knew that this was fear and so, had an idea up my sleeve. His care package was fully funded and had been sub-contracted to a nursing agency in Wood Green. The following day I went to the office and proposed to them that I be employed as his senior nurse and that I could manage his care, as well as his 'challenging' behaviour. They almost bit my hand off and, almost immediately I was on the job. Michael's care was shared between agencies who took responsibility for different things. He had traditional district nursing support for his terminal care, including medicine, however his HIV and AIDS care was managed by an organisation called ACET who were very skilled in that specialty, thank goodness. We organised a new rota so that my sisters could spend some time with their children, I was there every day as a nurse, and we also had daily support from district nurses and night nurses plus family members who were still sleeping over every night.

As time went on and he slowly deteriorated, everyone was becoming very tired and stressed on some level. I had only been involved for a few weeks but everyone else had been giving one-hundred-and-ten-per cent for months so we were beginning to wonder when it was going to end, indeed I had a feeling that Michael was so comfortable with all of us around him that he didn't want to go (this would be confirmed by Dr Patrick Dixon near the end).

Due to the levels of stress combined with the Scottish survival instinct, we spent a lot of time gathered in the living-room area laughing. People would arrive for a visit and would end up in hysterics, often with Michael included. When he was so emaciated and he laughed, his teeth looked huge which made us laugh more. Even when we thought he was sleeping and we were chatting, every so often he would keep us on our toes with an interjection, 'Naw, that's no true!' or 'Aye, I remember that' which made us all aware of what we said in his company. Even though he was almost completely blind, he could still see some outlines or shadows. I remember one day he was sleeping, and I was sitting by his bed when our friend Stephen Hadfield stood in the doorway, and rather than speak and wake Michael, he signalled to ask if I wanted a cup of tea. Michael immediately said, "Is that you, Stephen?" Stephen looked shocked.

"How the hell did you know that was me!" he replied.

"Because when you stand up you hold one shoulder higher than the other!" came his firm response, making Stephen self-conscious, attempting to straighten up his posture!

As the weeks began to drag, and Michael was still with us, we were beginning to feel exhausted. As Easter approached, I remember saying to Michael one day, "Listen, Michael, if you're not gone by Good Friday, I'm outta here!" with a dry laugh.

"Aw fuck off you!" he said with his teeth smiling over his blanket. He did deteriorate to a point where I wondered what was keeping him alive. He was no longer eating, was having very little fluids and yet his kidneys were producing plenty of urine and his heart was still pumping strongly, however one evening I noticed that he was screaming out in pain if he was touched and was generally unsettled. I called the team at ACET and they suggested I remove the syringe driver, but I protested because I felt that he was suffering, and I didn't want him to leave this life in pain. At that point they said that they would send a doctor to see us and a couple of hours later Dr Patrick Dixon arrived at the top of the stairs. I explained what had happened and that we were all keen that he was comfortable and pain free. He asked if we could all gather in Michael's room, so everyone was rounded up and we sat around the bed whilst Patrick sat on the bed holding Michael's hand. He then commended us all for the commitment and love we had shown Michael and how special it was. He then asked us to imagine how he must be feeling.

"Can you imagine standing on the edge of a cliff, surrounded by so much love, not knowing what is on the other side and being frightened and all the people who you love are telling you to jump? Where would you rather be? He knows he has to go but he wants to stay here with you. Let him know that you love him and that he can go in his own time, that there's no rush."

Everyone in the room was deeply affected by his words and tears started to flow. We thanked him for his wisdom and showed him out, then we individually had some time with Michael and did what he suggested. I remember saying, "Sorry for pushing you, son, it was really selfish of me. I love you and I'm here for as long as you need." It was amazing how the atmosphere changed following that meeting although it was later that evening when he decided to go, after everyone had made peace with him.

The night nurse came running into the living room and said, "He's going now." So we all ran through to the bedroom and surrounded him as he drew his last breaths. After all the stress and trauma, it was a beautiful end for him, and for us as there was nothing left unsaid and we were all present.

A few days later he was cremated following a service at Mildmay Hospital and then his ashes were taken home to Denny for burial. As I breathed a sigh of relief that it was over, I didn't realise just how lost and traumatised I was feeling.

Peter

It was late in 1985 and I was sitting in The George IV in Ida Street, Poplar, with Michael Kelly and a few other friends. The George was a large pub and a hub for the local East End LGBT community and was instrumental in raising much needed funds for HIV and AIDS research and treatment. We would work very hard to put on full musical-comedy drag shows to raise money for THT or Lighthouse. The shows were funny, outrageous, well written and well directed by Spike Rhodes who was a prominent drag entertainer at the time. We did shows like Chicago, Leader of The Pack and The Sound of Mucus to name a few, rehearsing on weekday evenings for weeks and then performing every night over a long weekend to packed houses.

Michael Kelly and myself loved the fun and laughter of being involved in such big productions and I still remember the hysteria when he played Gretel from The Sound of Mucus in a blue gingham dress left over from Dorothy in The Wizard of Oz, 'Well we ain't in fucking Kansas now Toto!' along with black suede T-bar high heels and a dark wig with pigtails and a fringe. I played Liesl, the oldest Von Trapp child, so we were often rushing on and off stage together. I can still see him, during one performance, rushing down the step to the changing room when his T-Bar heel caught on the top step and he went down like a sack of King Edwards, ending up at the foot of the small staircase with his leg halfway up his back and the T-bar nowhere to be seen! We were meant to be changing costumes to go back on for the next number, but we just couldn't stop laughing. Every time I looked at his face, with his wig slightly squinted by the fall and him hobbling with one shoe, I was a basket case! I don't know how we managed to get through the next number, but when he said Gretel's one line, "Why don't I feel better?" the whole cast disintegrated in a heap of laughter, as did the audience who had witnessed his fall.

The GIVE (George IV Entertains) company were quite a close-knit bunch who looked out for each other and generally got on very well. Naturally, there were always a few dramas going on if you needed them, but the AIDS crisis was unbelievably traumatic and difficult to comprehend which meant we really needed each other. As I write this, Covid-19 sweeps the world and I think back to those times and the lack of support and understanding from most quarters, for what was believed to be a gay plague, which the tabloid press regularly reported didn't affect anyone else. If it hadn't been for organisations like Terrence Higgins Trust, Mildmay Mission and Lighthouse there would have been no services at all.

One of the most exciting things which happened to us at the time was being invited to The Hippodrome, Leicester Square, (formerly the night club The Talk of The Town) to provide some outrageous glamour on a special cabaret night. A gang of us got together a load of costumes and headed to Leicester Square, where we were shown to the basement where the dressing rooms were.

When Peter Stringfellow took over, he maintained the hydraulic stage, so every night there was a fantastic light show, then half of the dance floor would rise up to form the stage; then the centre of the stage would disappear and come back up with the star of the show ready to perform. It was a fantastic way to build up the tension and excitement and I saw many fantastic acts on that stage. We were all downstairs ready, in the loudest and most glitzy costumes, laughing our heads off when the stage manager came down and asked us to come up on stage and just strike poses on a gallery behind the stage whilst the cabaret was performing, we would be looking at the audience from behind the act. We went upstairs and got into position as the light show was happening, then we stood in our positions and watched the stage go down to bring up the surprise cabaret, the compere built up the tension before saying, "Ladies and gentleman, Miss Eartha Kitt!" I thought I was going to be sick because she was one of my favourite performers and I couldn't believe I was going to be only a few feet away from her. As the stage appeared there she was, as always, lying on a chez longue, making purring sounds. We were supposed to be standing still, but I wanted to watch! She'd recently had a major resurgence in the London club-scene so the bass was thumping for her dance hit Where is my man. She slid off the couch and started performing, and I could see the audience go wild with her sexy antics. What a woman, what a life-lived, what a performer!

So anyway, I was sitting at a table with Michael and a few others when I noticed a stranger in the vicinity, a young black guy with a relaxed perm wearing jeans and a leather jacket. "Who's that?" I quickly asked Michael.

"Oh, I've never seen him before son, he looks your type tae!" came the loud reply in order to be heard over the music.

After getting eye contact and smiling a few times, a pint of Lager and a vodka appeared on the table. Henry the barman said in his gorgeous Irish accent, "It's from that fella there." He pointed across the room. "He asked what you drink, so I told him lager and vodka!" I thanked Henry then looked across and raised my glass in acknowledgement of the gesture. Before long I was standing with him at the bar. His name was Peter, he worked in finance and he lived on the Stratford Leytonstone border close to Thatched House. He was born in Jamaica but came over here as a child to join his mother who had moved to the UK to find work. We connected quickly and were enjoying the conversation. I asked him why he hadn't been in before and he said he'd only just heard about it and was on his way home from work in St James Park so thought he would pop in and see. As it got later, I could see Michael getting drunker and holding court with the crowd at the table, laughter flowing loudly.

Peter suggested going for some food so I suggested a little-known Chinese restaurant known locally as The Steps which was in an old undeveloped part of the docklands but made beautiful food for a very reasonable price. The house's hostess was an English lady called Bina who was married to the owner. She was a force to be reckoned with who dressed in traditional Chinese tunic tops, and wore heavy eye make-up to help her look more Asian, but she was great fun and very funny. We sat at a small table with a lazy Susan in the middle and had a variety of Chinese and Cantonese dishes, talking for what seemed hours, but being regularly joined by Bina who I knew from my time at the Oliver Twist restaurant in Leman Street. This was a restaurant which other restauranteurs used to go to after they had closed, as it stayed open later. But it wasn't licensed, so you had to take your own wine.

We then headed back to his place in Stratford for more drinks, and suffice to say I stayed the night. I had been single for a little while but I had a feeling I was going to see Peter again before too long. A couple of days later I was working in the Leman Street restaurant under the new owners, and Peter walks in. One of the advantages of not having mobile phones back then was that people had to make an effort to arrange dates, or to find someone you had only met briefly. I felt my face light-up when I saw him. "What are you doing here?" I asked with a smile.

"I remembered you said your restaurant was in Leman Street, so I thought I'd have a look for it," he said.

"Oh, that's nice. I wasn't sure if I would see you again," I said, fishing for a compliment. He smiled broadly and said, "I wouldn't go to all this trouble for just anyone!" He pulled out a stool at the bar.

This was the start of a really fiery and passionate relationship. Within a few weeks I had moved into his place in Stratford and we were very much in love, I would say for my part probably for the first time. Our relationship was strong but turbulent, as he suffered from bouts of depression which could be very dark at times, and would occasionally lead to him not coming home because he had been arrested, usually whilst standing in a depressed trance, and charged with loitering. It was during this time that I realised how differently young black men were treated from young white men. I have never been pulled over by police when I have been in a car with a white driver but on a number of occasions, I have had to sit in the passenger seat whilst my black friends were stopped and searched or breathalysed. After living together for a couple of happy years, and still very much in love, he hit a major depression. We had been in Scotland visiting family earlier in the year, and we'd had a lovely time, but when we got back he didn't really return to his normal routine. By this time I had started working as a community psychiatric nurse, and one day I came home for lunch to find him curled-up in the foetal position on the bathroom floor. I sat down beside him with my back against the bath and gently rubbed his back. "What's up, Peter?" I asked gently.

He began to sob, saying, "I don't want to be here anymore. I just can't do it." I held him for a while, reassuring him that he would be OK and that we should see a doctor, but he was inconsolable. I couldn't bear to see him so broken and not be able to fix him, so over the next few days I tried every strategy to lift his mood and got exasperated by his refusal to see a doctor or counsellor or to be able to make, even a small effort to help himself. I had never seen him like that before.

Eventually I lost the plot as his suicidal ideation became constant, so I screamed at him, "Right! Let's fucking do it together, because you're not leaving me to clean up all this mess, and if you're not here then I don't want to fucking be here either!" I saw his expression change and he appeared shocked at my suggestion.

"Are you serious?" he asked in disbelief.

"Yes, I fucking am! Why should you be able to check-out and leave me with all your shit? It's not fair, Peter, you're not even making an effort!" I roared at him. He sat up straight and stared ahead of him.

"I'm sorry, Mike, I'll try a bit more," he whispered as his bottom lip trembled. I loved him so much and had no intention of killing myself, I was trying my best to give him a reason to stay. I spent the next few days observing him, popping home at lunchtimes and coming straight home in the evenings. He was a little better but still very low. The following week I came home from work just after five, and as I opened the front door, I smelt cooking. I closed the door and walked up the hall towards the kitchen, the place looked spotless and everywhere was vacuumed. As I entered the kitchen, there was Peter showered, dressed in nice jeans and a casual shirt, cooking spicy food at the cooker. The table was laid for two, with a candle in the middle, wine and a vase of flowers. He smiled at me and approached with a smile before kissing me and holding me in a bear-hug for a few seconds.

"Have I died and gone to Heaven? What have you done with Peter?" I said sarcastically and we both laughed. I hadn't seen him laugh for so long.

Again, I questioned him, "What's going on, Peter?" Not fully believing what was before me.

"I just woke up this morning and felt better," he said. "So I cleaned up the house and decided I would give you a nice surprise as I've put you though the mill these last few weeks, and it's not fair. I'm sorry I've been so bad to live with, you must hate me."

"If I hated you, I wouldn't be here, Peter," I said as he pulled out a chair for me at the table. I sat down at the circular table, which my sister Alice had brought when she and Errol moved down from Scotland and noticed a small gift-box sitting in my place. "What's this?" I said as I held up the small box.

"Open it," Peter said with an excited smile. I pulled the lid open expecting to see a ring because of the size of the box, but it wasn't a ring, it was a car-key with the Ford logo on the fob. I looked at him with a puzzled expression and he signalled to me to follow him back down the hall to the front door. He opened the door and pointed to the road just outside our gate. There, sat a brand-new, metallic blue, Ford Sierra, gleaming in the sunlight. He was so excited to show me the car, opening the doors and explaining the features. I had only just started driving lessons and knew nothing about cars.

"I can't drive, Peter," I laughed.

He replied, "It's for us both and once you pass your test you can use it for work as I commute any way." I was shocked but delighted by the thoughtfulness of the gesture. We went back inside and I hugged him tight.

"Thanks, Peter, I love you," I said, hoping that I finally had him back from his depressive bout.

"I love you too. Now let's eat!" he said as he began placing starters on the table.

We had the most beautiful meal, which lasted most of the evening because we were chatting and laughing between courses and drinking lots of wine of course. We finished eating and the table was cleared when a bolt of lightning hit me out of the blue. My mental health training kicked back-in and I shouted, "Holy fuck!"

He was startled by my sudden outburst and said, "What is it, Mike? What's wrong?"

I looked him right in the eye and said, "You're gonna kill yourself, aren't you?"

Looking at him, it was like watching something deflate. His smile disappeared, his shoulders dropped, he began to cry and say, "I wanted you to be happy before I left, I don't want to hurt you." He sobbed.

"Peter!" I yelled. "How long did you think I would be happy for after you killed yourself?" I couldn't believe what he had planned and went into overdrive trying to make the house safe. I went around the house trying to find anything which could be harmful. Ligatures, knives, screwdrivers, pills and started hiding them in safe places. Peter just sat in the kitchen sobbing.

"I'm sorry, Mike, I love you but I'm sorry," he kept repeating through his tears. Finally, I thought I had hidden everything with potential for harm when I noticed the car keys. 'Oh fuck' I thought as I went into the bedroom and found a toilet bag, hid the keys in a zipper compartment and then the bag underneath our washing pile in the basket. Comfortable that everything was now safe I returned to console Peter who was still sitting at the kitchen table.

"Come to bed, Peter," I said quietly. "It's getting late and we both need some sleep." He stood up silently and I put my arm around his shoulders leading him through to the bedroom. He sat on the side of the bed, dissociated and staring into space. "Get undressed, Peter," I said. "You need some sleep and so do I. I've got work in the morning."

I helped him undress and cover him in the duvet, then I climbed in beside him and snuggled up with my arm tightly around him. "You'll be ok. We'll sort this," I whispered as I heard his breathing slow down and hoped he was falling asleep.

I would have to try and stay awake as I knew he was in a very bad place. Occasionally I nodded off but would wake up with a start and panic, but he was still there, until I dozed off and woke at six-thirty and he was gone. I jumped out of bed and ran to the kitchen and bathroom and around the house but there was no sign of him. I checked my hiding places and nothing was missing, then I went to find the car keys and they were gone. He had removed them from the bag and replaced it under the washing.

I sat on the side of the bed and knew it was over. I had lost and he was gone. I lay back down on the bed, knowing that there was nothing I could do to stop him in a city the size of London. He could be anywhere. I began to cry silent tears as, once again, my life came crashing down around me.

I showered and went to work as I didn't know what else to do and, at around ten-thirty, I got a phone call to say he had been found in an underground carpark with a hosepipe attached to the exhaust. I hung up the phone and sat at my desk staring into space. My colleague Ben came over and asked if I was OK. I had only worked there for a short time and hadn't shared any of my personal life with them. "My boyfriend, Peter, is dead," I said. "He's gassed himself in the car."

Ben was shocked and said, "Oh my God, let me speak to Jacques, you have to go home, Mike." He rushed out of the office. They both returned and were very supportive asking if they could do anything, if I needed anything, etcetera, I refused any help and just said that I had to go but I would be in touch. As I walked down the wooden stairs from my office I met Phil.

"What are you up to?" she said with a smile, unaware of my situation.

"I'm just going home, Phil," I said. "I've just had some bad news."

She came rushing over and said, "What is it, Mike? Tell me please, you look worried." I told her my news and she was shocked and surprised. "Where are you going now?" she asked.

I looked at my watch and said, "The North Star. I need a drink!" Because of the laws at that time, I had no legal rights. His family, who were at the core of his problems because they couldn't accept his sexuality, were next of kin so I was not included in any funeral arrangements or, indeed, invited to the funeral, such was the shame that they carried about their son's sexuality. I had no fight left in me so simply left the house and got a flat with Michael Kelly. The support I got from Michael, my sisters and my friends was great, and Phil McCoy was particularly active in supporting me because I worked with her.

A few days after Peter's death I got a phone call in my office from Phil, who knew that his family had closed ranks and were keeping me out of the loop. I didn't even know if he had been buried yet which was a terrible feeling. "Meet me in The North

Star at five, I have some news," she said very secretively. I did what she asked and at five p.m., there she was, in the corner of the pub, alone with two pints of lager.

"What is it?" I asked frantically as I gulped down my drink.

"I've done some digging and I know where Peter is. I can't find anything out about the funeral arrangements, but his body is in Selby's funeral home if you want to go and see him. His family are arriving for prayers at seven so we really need to go now so that they don't see you." I couldn't thank her enough and we rushed down our drinks and headed down to Selby's.

The funeral attendant was very nervous when we arrived but had agreed to the visit with Phil.

"You will have to be very quick, no more than ten minutes, as I've been given strict instructions not to let you in," he said in an anxious tone.

"Thank you so much," I said, as he ushered us into a side room. I entered the dimly lit room where sombre organ music played in the background, and I saw the dark mahogany coffin in the middle of the room.

"I'll just be outside if you need me," the man said kindly.

Slowly, I approached the coffin, praying that it wasn't him but then I saw his hair and his beautiful face. I felt a torrent of energy flow through my body and my tears began to flow. I held on to the side of the coffin to keep myself standing upright as I felt my body begin to falter. I stared at Peter, still and expressionless and wished he would open his eyes. I didn't want to be left alone, and beneath my grief and sadness, I felt immense rage that he had left me. He was dressed in a black dress-suit with satin lapels, a white shirt and a small bowtie with white gloves, which were very smart but not at all Peter. I started to cry loudly and said, "Look at you! They don't even know you! You should be wearing jeans and a fuckin' sweat-shirt!" I wailed through my tears. "Look at those gloves! You look like fuckin' Mickey Mouse!" is all I could think of when I looked at his clasped hands. The attendant came in and said, "You'll have to be quick, they'll be here soon." So I pulled myself together and stood quietly, praying that he was safe on the other side and that he had found peace. The attendant knocked on the door and I kissed Peter goodbye, knowing that I would never see him again, my warm tears running down his cold face.

As I hit the night air on Leytonstone High Road, I let out a roar like a wounded animal and cried like a baby, sliding down a wall and sitting on the ground weeping. Phil was crying and leaned down over me. "Come on, Mike, we have to go. If they arrive all hell will break loose." She helped me up and we slowly walked the short distance to Lincoln's for a few drinks. I really appreciated Phil McCoy that night as I felt completely at a loss and didn't know how I was going to move forward without Peter. She was very gentle and understanding of my trauma, not demanding anything, just being with me and I appreciated it, but most importantly she knew that I needed to say goodbye and she made it happen.

I very soon moved out of the house as I couldn't bear to be amongst his belongings when his mother came to collect everything. They were entitled to the house so I knew they would have thrown me out anyway. My sisters and nephew were tenants upstairs so legally they could stay but his mother made it a vicious battle and terrorised them before they were re-housed. She truly was a horrible woman and when I saw her nasty, vindictive behaviour, I understood, at last, why Peter was so emotionally unstable.

Barbados

Celebrate endings – for they precede new beginnings.
—Jonathan Lockwood Huie

In 1989, the Conservative government conducted an exercise called Clinical Re-grading within the NHS but which was an entirely separate and self-reliant body. Up to this point there was an agreed pay-scale for every grade of work no matter where you lived in the country, except London, you were paid the same rate. This meant that, as a charge nurse in Glasgow I would be on the same pay-scale as a charge nurse in Sheffield. This system was generally fair, but as far as the government were concerned it helped to maintain unity amongst nurses so it had to be re-structured. How could they privatise the NHS if the nurses stood together and fought them? It was the most divisive strategy I had ever seen. Nurses who had worked together on the same wards and departments were given different grades, so people doing the same jobs, for the first time, had different salaries. As a trade union official at the time, I was called to many wards and departments where long-time colleagues were almost coming to blows because of the unfairness of the grades. This was the pivotal moment when Thatcher succeeded in 'dividing and conquering' the solidarity of nurses. I spent a long time preparing and launching appeals against grades for many people, most of which were unsuccessful. I myself, as a community nurse, was automatically awarded a G-grade, which was a reasonable increase and was backdated to April, so I had a lump-sum to look forward to.

When it arrived in my account around November, I was determined not to let it simply disappear on bills and such, so I decided to look up an old friend I knew from the days of Oliver Twist, to see where she was in the world. Diane was an American travel-rep, and I met her when she started bringing groups of American tourists to Oliver Twist for dinner evenings. We became good friends, and often went out partying and clubbing, and I would often stay in her suite at The Tower Hotel. I managed to track her travels and discovered that she was in Barbados. I called her apartment one evening and told her I was thinking of visiting her, so she screamed the place down and said, "Yeah please come, Michael! You can stay here, I have two rooms!" The next day I went to a travel agent and booked a flight with Pan Am flying via Miami the following week. I had never done a transatlantic flight so was quite excited, but a little nervous at the prospect as it wasn't long after the Lockerbie disaster when a Pan Am flight was bombed.

I remember getting to the airport early, checking-in and starting to drink as I waited for my gate number to be called. The plane was not busy so there was plenty of space if I had wanted to lie down; however I was too busy drinking to think about sleep. I sat towards the back of the plane and got to know the cabin-crew who were full of mischief and laughter, as they weren't too busy. At Miami airport I changed to a BWIA flight which took me directly to Barbados where Diane was to be waiting at arrivals. The feeling when I stepped out of the plane door and down the steps onto the tarmac was amazing, the wind was warm and the sunlight so bright. I could hardly believe that little old me had found his way to the West Indies! This was going to be a great holiday, I could feel it in my bones.

I heard Diane before I saw her as she had a voice like a foghorn. "Michael!" she called in a sharp American accent as she ran towards me. We hugged and she said, "Welcome to Barbados, let's get you home!" After a ten-minute journey, where I looked at every palm tree, sandy beach and rum-shop, we arrived at Kingsway Apartments, on Maxwell Coast Road.

I carried my bags through a bar area to a back courtyard, where several apartments were located. Diane's was furthest away on the first floor, accessed via an external staircase. It was a basic, but bright and airy apartment with sliding French doors. We sat down and had a couple of drinks from my duty-free stash before jumping in the shower and getting dressed to go out for dinner. As we walked back through the bar, which was quite busy, Diane shouted loudly, "Everyone! This is my friend Michael who will be staying with me for a few weeks!"

And I heard a chorus of, "Hi, Michael! Welcome to Kingsway!" There was one woman in particular who stood out from the rest, being particularly direct and noisy, and who I immediately thought I would try to avoid. Her name was Patricia, and we went on to become lifelong friends. We drove to a bar called The Ship, where Diane knew everyone, and we had some food and a few more drinks, chatting enthusiastically about everything we had done since we last met in London. When we returned to Kingsway the bar was a bit quieter, and there was a couple of barstools free, so we grabbed them and sat down. The Umpire's Inn was an open-air bar which was sub-let by Kingsway to David Archer; a well-known cricket umpire. It had a tall bar and a few tables and chairs sitting on a patio area. We ordered some drinks and I started chatting to David, who was a very funny man and could tell a good story. There was an English couple sitting at the bar called Dave and Rita who drove a blue Ford Escort from the 1970s. They also became good friends with me over the years, then I heard a commotion approaching and it was once again Patricia. She said, "Hi!" and pulled up a barstool next to me and Diane. She looked directly at me and, in a low voice said, "I invited a friend of mine from Martha's Vineyard to come visit and she's driving me fucking nuts! Everything about her is false; and I keep finding hair extensions, false nails and all kinds of other shit lying all over the place!" I began to laugh and started to think that I quite liked this American, she was funny!

Very soon afterwards, a middle-aged woman with long black hair arrived at the bar and Patricia nudged me and whispered, "That's her."

She stood at the bar and said to David, "I'm having terrible sinus problems, can you recommend a drink that might help as I'm drowning in my saliva." I looked at Pat, Diane and David and we all started to laugh at the same time. Lisa then sat with us and, although very pleasant, she did nothing but moan and complain about everything. After a time she said, "Oh, I feel awful, I'm gonna call it a night and go to bed."

There was a collective sigh of relief as she walked towards the courtyard area and everyone said, "Goodnight!"

Patricia then began to launch into a tirade about how awful she had been throughout the holiday and that their friendship would not survive. David suddenly handed me a rum and said, "You better have this before you drown in your saliva!" and the place went into uproar! I sat at that bar every night for three weeks, getting to know all the regulars and laughing most of the time. We all went into Bridgetown one evening, to the Harbourside, to see a jazz singer called Cece backed by a jazz pianist called Ernie Small. She was wonderful, a real talent, and he was one of those seasoned and wise musicians who just felt his way through every piece of music. They were having a break and I noticed Lisa approach Ernie and start chatting with him. When the second half started, he announced a guest singer and up walked Lisa to the small stage area. He played her song's intro and she began to sing with the most beautiful, deep, jazz voice. I couldn't believe how stunning her voice was. The audience loved it too, so she sang a couple more before returning to the table.

"You're a dark horse, Lisa, that was amazing!" I said.

"I used to be a jazz singer before I met my husband," she said. "He is a judge and didn't like me singing in clubs, so I stopped." At that moment I could see why she was so unhappy and had become a moaner and complainer. Music made her come to life, smile and communicate in a very special way.

"You need to dump him and go back on the road," I said with a smile, but she simply shrugged her shoulders.

Barbados was to become my island home and I visited whenever an opportunity arose. On my second trip, I was sitting outside Kingsway having a drink with Patricia when I saw a tall, handsome Bajan walk along Maxwell Coast Road pushing a trolley with an oil-drum converted into a barbeque. He stopped and asked if we would like anything, so we rallied the troops, put some music on and he started cooking for us. We had a great evening and I noticed Patricia had a little crush on the barbeque guy, whose name was Salty. They started seeing each other and were a really good fit, her need to caretake matched by his need to be looked after. I was sitting at the bar one night with Patricia who was due to return soon to Martha's Vineyard. "What are you going to do about Salty?" I asked.

"Oh God, I wish I knew, Michael. I really like him, but there are no black people on the Vineyard, and it would cause such a furore if I took him back with me," she said sadly.

"Fuck them!" I said. "I wouldn't give a fuck what anyone said or thought about it. It's none of their business! If you want to be with him, you should take him back with you and hold your head high!"

She looked at me sheepishly and said, "Do you think?"

"Yes!" I screamed, "You clearly love each other, Pat, and he's very handsome, so there's a risk that if you don't take him now someone else will claim him whilst you are at home!"

I saw her brain calculating the various outcomes of each decision, then she looked at me and said, "You're right!" and ordered some more drinks to celebrate. When Salty arrived, she asked him if he would like to return to the US with her and he excitedly said yes. "I've always wanted to go to the USA!" he kept saying, "I gonna make you so happy, Patrice!" They were married the following year on Maxwell beach and Salty became a permanent resident of Martha's Vineyard. I went to visit them one year on The Vineyard and was delighted to see a sign outside the front of her house which said 'Salty's Place'.

Martha's Vineyard is a beautiful island a few miles off the coast of Massachusetts. It was the setting for the fictional Amity Island in the original Jaws movie, and Spielberg and his crew were there for months, shooting with their famous mechanical shark. It was also home to Jackie Onassis, James Cagney, James Taylor and Carly Simon. It is a stunning location with quaint wooden buildings built to look out to see for whalers returning home. The sitting US president usually holidays there every year as well, so my friend Pat made a fair sum of money every year by renting her home to the Secret Service protecting the president of the United States. Pat's house was lovely, and she built it following her divorce settlement. It was a two-storey villa with a full balcony out the back and a cellar below, close to the town of Vineyard Haven. Whilst there we were taken around the islands sights, including the main sets for Jaws which was instantly recognisable, but also to the famous Chappaquiddick Bridge where Edward Kennedy crashed his car, drowning his passenger Mary Jo Kopechne, before fleeing the scene in 1969.

We also visited the Native American Reservation sites where they had been forced to live by the government. I have always been interested in the spirituality and culture of the Native Americans. Unlike the negative racist portrayal as savages in cowboy movies, they are a peace-loving people whose relationship with animals and the earth as a whole is all encompassing. They understand the connection between everything that lives and breathes on earth and how important it is to keep a balance in all we do. They have always been truly holistic in their ways, long before it became fashionable. I found it deeply sad that this amazing group of people were kept on reservations and survived by making crafts and gifts for tourists. There had been so much generational trauma, passed down through their community, that alcohol and drug addiction had become commonplace, similarly with the Native Aboriginal people in Australia.

My love for Barbados continued year on year, however my addiction was progressing and I was finding it harder and harder to pull myself back together after a binging episode. I wasn't a true binger, I was more of a daily drinker, but I wasn't always pissed-up, however holidays were a different equation, especially on an island like Barbados which is soaked in rum. One of the best gifts for an alcoholic is permission to drink whenever they feel like it and a holiday in the Caribbean does exactly that, give permission. In the '80s and early '90s it was a common practice to see people sitting in rum-shops playing dominoes from early morning, with a flask of rum and water on the table. People just stayed topped-up all day.

An example of that was an elderly Canadian woman called Margaret who spent her winters on the south coast. I met her in Kingsway Apartments as she spent her day driving between rum shops topping-up. She would get a shot of the cheapest rum and place a dollar on the bar, then she would dilute with water and sip it. Although she didn't look it she must have been pissed for most of the day, even when driving around the island. She gave me a lift one day and I was grateful to survive to tell the tale. She was a loud and aggressive driver for such an old woman, but sometimes she drove slowly as she was quite drunk. If a driver came up behind her she would hang out of the window and scream, "Stop fucking tailgating me you goddamn Bajan asshole!" They would then overtake and beep their horns angrily and she would look at me and say, "See what I mean about this fucking island?" Having said that, unbeknownst to her, she was a major source of my entertainment as she was extremely funny to just observe. She had clearly had some cosmetic surgery over the years as she must have been around seventy-five or eighty years old at the time but looked between sixty-five and seventy, I would say. I remember sitting in the bar one evening with Pat and the famous cricketer Everton Weekes who became a good friend of mine and who was also very funny.

He leaned over to me and whispered with a wry smile, "Do you think Margaret's had some work done?"

"Work done?" I exclaimed. "She's been pulled so tight her pubic hair is between her breasts!" At that point, Everton sprayed his mouthful of drink all over the table and choked on his laughter.

When he finally regained his composure and through continued laughter, he kept repeating, "You a bad man, Delaney! You gonna kill me!"

Everton was a good friend of David's through the cricketing world and he came almost every day to have a drink. He could tell a story that man, and when he came to the punchline, he would flick his fingers together as he delivered it and roar with laughter. He only died recently, at home in Barbados, at around ninety years old.

The owner of Kingsway was a man called Charles Briggs who lived on site, with his British girlfriend, but he was also helped in running things by his parents. He was a big, imposing gentleman who was never very comfortable around me due to my, at times, outrageous behaviour whilst I was holding court in the bar. Many years later, when Kingsway was long gone and the Bougainvillea hotel stood proudly opposite the site, I met him with Patricia. He called my name and gave me the biggest hug ever. I was quite shocked and said, "Charles, have you had therapy? You never used to like me!"

He took a breath and said, "You know, I learned a lot since then. I was scared of you and that was silly!" And he gave me a bear-hug just to make sure I knew. I was very touched by his honesty in that moment, as I could remember how he used to freeze when I was around.

One of the major warnings that I needed to get a grip on my drinking was when flying back to London one year. There was a ritual at that time where a gang of us would accompany someone to the airport, a couple of hours before they were due to be there. There was a rum shop nearby which did great food, then we would all pile over to the open-air bar at the airport and from there we could wave people off. When it was my turn, it had been a particularly rum-fuelled few weeks so, as I waved everyone off and boarded the plane, I was looking forward to taking off and getting a few more drinks down me for the eight hour flight. I was flying BWIA, and as commonly occurred at the time, there was some engine trouble, so we were held on the runway for over an hour whilst some work was done. I could feel my whole body begin to go into withdrawals as we sat there, and this caused my anxiety to make things feel even worse. Eventually we took off and, before we had even climbed to cruising altitude, I was buzzing for cabin crew. After a few minutes a pleasant lady arrived, looked at me and said, "You need a drink?"

"Yes, please," I said shakily. "I'll have six vodkas and two cokes for starters please!"

She gave a loud laugh and said, "Coming right up!" Moments like that were the signals that I was physically dependent, but once they had passed, I never thought of them again. As the old saying goes, "Denial is not just a river in Egypt."

Pennycress

After a few weeks of being allowed half-days out of treatment to find accommodation, and not getting anywhere suitable in Bristol or Bath, I was forced to resign myself to the reality that I would have to try looking in Weston-super-Mare. This was not what I wanted to hear, but Graham my counsellor suggested I work on step three; make a decision to turn your will and your lives over to the care of God as you understood him. "Just go into Weston and see what happens, whatever will be, will be," he said hopefully on a rainy Monday.

Dejected and unenthusiastic I headed into Weston, and as I had no money to my name, I decided to try the Deposit Bond scheme, a charity which provided the guarantee of a required deposit amount to prospective landlords. Their office was in the YMCA building, and whilst waiting to be seen by Bernadette, the manager, I met Kevin, who was to become one of my closest and most loyal friends. Kevin had recently come out of another rehab in the area and had a small flat in town. We just connected immediately and arranged to meet when I got out the following week.

After filling in forms and handing them in I was told that I had been approved for the deposit bond, but not only that, if I was interested they could show me a new, one bed flat which was available on the Locking Castle Estate a couple of miles outside of town. After a couple of weeks of trudging around Bristol and Bath I couldn't believe my luck and Bernadette immediately drove me to the flat for a viewing. It was a beautiful apartment in a small three storey block with intercom security doors. Very clean and well-appointed as they say, but with absolutely no furnishings at all. I didn't care. For the second time on my journey so far, when I worked step three and let go of control, everything worked out for me. At last, I had a new place to call my own and somewhere to make a fresh start. Excitedly, I scampered back to Broadway Lodge to share my good fortune with my fellow peers and counsellors. "This programme shit really works," I said rather excitedly as I described my unexpected afternoon of meeting new friends and getting a flat!

I had a few days left to finish up some assignment work I still had to do before dealing with the end of my five months of safety and security within Broadway Lodge. How could I ever thank them, not only for the unbelievable amount of work they had put me through, but for the loving way in which they had emotionally held me and nurtured me whilst I regained my physical and emotional strength. Leaving was a very difficult event for me, as I had always avoided the emotional pain of endings, but again I did what my counsellor suggested and worked through everything; leaving a week later with no regrets or resentments. I left extended care with a holdall and a black bin liner which contained all of my worldly possessions, but I felt so proud of myself, and hopeful that I could make this fresh start work for me. I said an emotional farewell to the people who had been my family and I headed out to Locking Castle.

When I arrived and entered my empty little flat I felt nervous but excited. I walked around the rooms imagining how I could make it look when I had some income and could afford artwork, curtains and furnishings. My little kitchenette was basic but very functional and my open plan lounge did not have space for a three piece suite, so I had to think about how best to furnish it. Having always been in work for the last twenty years, since I left school, I was unprepared for the benefits system as it was then. If the brutal regime of today's DWP (Department for Work and Pensions) and universal credit were in place, I doubt if I would have got past the first hurdle of relocating to a new town.

Due to the amount of rehabilitation facilities in the Weston area at that time, the Department for Social Security, the DSS, were well acquainted with the needs of vulnerable adults coming out of treatment and in need of some help. I however was absolutely stunned at the lack of support which was available to me because I had always worked. The days of related earnings had been stopped and I found myself fighting for every penny that I could get which eventually came to £30 per week from which I had to pay a 'top-up percentage' of council tax. Eventually I went to see my MP as the DSS would not give me income support because I was on Incapacity Benefit (this was why I got less money and had to pay extra taxes). After several letters back and forth between my MP and the DSS, I was awarded an extra pound per weekly income support, which gave me £31 per week to live on, but then I also got full council tax and housing benefits. Somehow, I managed to survive on this amount until I returned to full-time employment a year later.

It wasn't easy by any means, but it was easier than getting up every day and feeling suicidal at the thought of having to spend another day in active addiction and not being able to stop. My friend Kevin, who got £70 per week, always laughed when the subject of money came up and how resentful I was towards the DSS for the way they treated me. Another example of this bias was trying to get a furniture grant. I had a small apartment and needed basics like bed, sofa, dishes, saucepans etc. I was refused a grant and was given a crisis loan of £300 which had to be paid back from my benefits! People around me were getting grants right left and centre, but not little old me, I had to pay it back out of nothing! I really did have to learn how to manage my resentments!

The first few nights in my new place I spent on the floor with a borrowed sleeping bag and pillow, a radio-cassette recorder and a small milk pan, which heated soup as well as water for tea or coffee. I vividly remember lying on the floor in my sleeping bag listening to the radio as New Labour won the 1997 election and Tony Blair became Prime Minister. I was full of so much hope, and this change of government filled me with even more hope for everyone else. I lay there, on the floor, in the dark, with shadows coming through my curtainless windows, tearful but smiling, and singing Things Can Only Get Better. It felt as if the whole country was getting a fresh start.

With my crisis loan being what it was, on the advice of others in my situation, I went to a charity shop called Weston Hospice care and almost completely furnished my apartment with good quality second-hand furniture; including an almost new king-size orthopaedic bed and some nice sitting room chairs, not to mention a huge television set, coffee table and bookcase. My safe-space was coming together nicely and was starting to feel comfortable and homely. A few weeks after I moved in my sister Eileen, her husband Chris and son Elliott, drove down from London for a visit and brought some extras such as a stereo system, bedding and towels as well as some of my own possessions from London. Although anxious and fearful about what the future might hold, for the first time in many years, I also felt quite safe within my four walls and used to look around my little flat and smile to myself, tentatively proud of myself but too fearful to take anything for granted.

Within a few months my daughter Clare asked if she could move down to stay for a few months, so I spoke to my landlord to see if he had any larger properties available and was surprised to be offered a three-bedroomed house in Worle – a small village next door to Weston. It was an unfurnished mid-terrace house but it was in a quiet cul-de-sac and had front and back gardens. I jumped at the opportunity, although it meant that I had to pay more money so it was also time to look for a job, as I was exhausted with the whole benefits battle to get what I needed. Clare moved in, but almost immediately started a relationship with a young guy called Simon who was also in recovery. They moved-in together very quickly and Clare was soon expecting my first grandchild Toni. She decided to go back to Scotland to have the baby, so gave up her flat and job to move back with her Granny Margaret. I was on my own again in a three-bedroomed house, but as it happened my friend Michael Dunne had his Bristol flat burgled and no longer felt safe there, so he moved in with me and rented a room.

The evening before I moved from Pennycress to my new place, I sat in my little flat surrounded by boxes and was suddenly overwhelmed by feelings of anxiety and fear. I didn't understand why I was feeling like this and felt emotional with the sudden intensity of it. Panicking and tearful, I phoned my sponsor, "I don't know what's happening... I'm terrified!"

My sponsor told me to sit down and said, "Look around your room. Those walls have kept you safer than you've felt for many years. They've held you and allowed you to grow in confidence. They've heard you laugh as well as cry, and tomorrow you are leaving them to move somewhere new. Celebrate your time in your flat. Thank the space for keeping you safe and allow yourself to grieve the end of this chapter." This made absolute sense to me and immediately my anxiety began to settle and dissipate and I took my sponsor's advice and walked around each room, feeling thankful for the safety I had felt and the fun that I had experienced within its walls. Since then, I have done that in every house I have left, and it really helps with those feelings!

Barley Wood was a sixty-seven bed, sprawling addiction treatment facility which worked closely with the criminal justice system, probation service and various police forces. It was originally opened as a higher end alcohol facility attached to Broadway Lodge, but it wasn't surviving financially. It really was at the sharp-end of addiction work and was an amazing environment to learn your trade. At any one time there were four or five groups running, so a team of between eight and ten counsellors were needed. This department was managed by a lady called Amanda. There was also a lady called Rosalie who was the head nurse, but she was demoted following an incident, before I stepped into that position. The unit manager was a fragile and insecure lady called Janet who presided over a very punishing regime for the staff. At times the atmosphere and energy in the staff areas was toxic, and people were often anxious and worried about their positions. The CEO was a bit of a character and was known to favour certain staff so there were often a number of female employees jostling to be their favourite. There never seemed to be any money in the bank, and we were forever having our salaries delayed. Despite all of this, we did some amazing work in Barley Wood, and over twenty years later, I still meet people who came into treatment in a sorry state but managed to get with the programme and turn their lives around.

Michael Dunne worked in Barley Wood as a finance officer. Our friend Robert was a counsellor and initially I was a nurse-therapist before becoming a deputy unit manager. It was a very seductive regime, and without strong boundaries, would completely take over your life. I was enmeshed for a while and got easily caught-up in the politics of a large facility. Most of the counsellors were in recovery themselves, so their prior work experience was very limited. I was in the position of having a twenty-year professional career pre-recovery, so I could see things differently from some people. At one point a culture of threat started to develop at Barley Wood; staff members would be targeted at different times for trivial reasons, just to let them know that they were never indispensable. Prior to my arrival there had been a couple of high-profile tribunal cases, which the management won, so people were reluctant to complain. I remember when I was promoted to deputy unit manager, I started to sense that the management were turning against Robert who could be somewhat unpredictable at times and difficult to manage, however he did some very good work with complex and vulnerable offenders.

Then I got a call to ask if I could join the unit manager, the CEO and the deputy CEO in a meeting to discuss my friend and colleague Robert. I went downstairs to Room 13 where they were gathered and sat down with them. The three of them then proceeded to dismantle my friend piece by piece, citing examples of aggressive behaviour to other staff, bullying of staff and poor boundaries around patients. Once they had presented their case, they looked at me to join them on their vendetta, and to spearhead the plan to remove him. I sat in silence for a short time as they stared at me expectantly.

"OK," I said. "I understand what you are saying, and I can't disagree with the allegations which you are levelling against Robert. However, you three have to take some responsibility as you trained him! Everything he does, he does because you taught him, and he hasn't worked anywhere else to learn any differently. The things you complain of, I see each of you doing on a regular basis, so I will struggle to victimise him when you are also guilty." I looked at the unit manager and said, "How can you say he is aggressive and bullying when I have witnessed you screaming at people in the staff room? I cannot be a part of this madness."

At that point the meeting fell silent, and I heard a metaphorical cannon beginning to crank as it was pointed in my direction. I knew immediately that my openness and honesty had signed my death warrant. It would only be a matter of time before they would concoct a scenario with which to get me out. They carried on and sacked Robert, and then the perfect situation arose. Barley Wood had a sister centre in Norfolk which was very badly run, as the staff were inexperienced, it was common knowledge that illicit drugs were regularly smuggled onto the premises. One of the Barley Wood counsellors relapsed and was given a treatment bed in Norfolk. Terry was a good lad and I enjoyed working with him, so I was happy to help facilitate his treatment. I called him one night to see how he was doing, and he was quite upset because he heard that there were drugs on the premises. I asked him how he was managing the situation and he said he was staying in his room and not engaging with other patients. The next day I was in Barley Wood for the nine a.m. handover, and I shared with the staff my conversation with Terry and that, unsurprisingly, he claimed there were drugs in the building. The team who were present sighed and agreed that it was an ongoing problem, but unbeknown to me one of the senior managers had left the meeting and phoned the CEO to let him know what I had said. Instead of calling me and saying, 'Mike, how can we better tackle the regular smuggling of illicit substances', I was suspended from duty for 'Endangering human life' by not reporting illicit substances to police under the Misuse of Drugs Act, despite the fact that I did not work in that service and had no evidence or control over it whatsoever as it was in Norfolk, and I was in Bristol! This was the ludicrous allegation that they were going to try and sack me on, so I had to get ready for battle.

Eventually we reached a settlement agreement and I resigned from my position, reflected and re-grouped, ready for the next challenge.

A Very Barley Wood Xmas

It was Xmas Day 1999 and I was working the day-shift as a nurse therapist in Barley Wood. It was a beautiful sixty-seven bed building, once a luxurious country home, now a bustling centre full of alcohol and drug addicts trying to get their lives together, many of whom had arrived via the criminal justice system. It was a pressure cooker of pain and regret but was also often filled with love, and laughter.

Xmas is very special in rehab, although also very painful for many. It brings up the countless losses of previous years, and the shame of addictive behaviour, making residents face their past and deal with the consequences, but it also shows that one can enjoy fun and laughter without the need for drugs or drink. A difficult balance for many to manage without a lot of practice.

By one p.m. all the groups were done, dinner had been served and around fifty residents were nervously awaiting family and friends arriving from various parts of the country. You could feel the excitement, mixed with fear and dread, as most of them had been 'bang at it' for years and had lost the trust of everyone up to that point. The large lounge was laid out with soft drinks and snacks for visitors and staff were ready to search bags and witness parcels being opened as the smuggling of illicit substances could cause havoc in a centre.

One of the important considerations on a day like today was to closely observe those who *did not* have visitors as this can be overwhelming, and very difficult for them to manage, and can compound feelings of worthlessness and isolation. By two p.m. the building was buzzing with visitors all trying to find a space to sit and chat with their loved ones, but with so many residents, plus families, it was a tight squeeze. It was around this time that I was in the packed lounge when I spotted one of the clients, with no visitors, having a full-blown panic attack. I squeezed through the crowd and took his arm, reassured him and asked him to follow me out to the reception area and through to the counsellors' offices.

David had been sent into rehab from the city of Liverpool, who were piloting a scheme to treat drug-using offenders rather than giving out custodial sentences. They were given an opportunity to change their behaviours instead of prison and this included a requirement for clean drug screens and good behaviour whilst in treatment. It helped many individuals to turn their lives around and become productive members of society.

David was a tall, quiet young man, not full of prison bravado, more reserved and introverted. We had little background information on him other than that he was a heroin addict and had been convicted of some drug related thefts and had taken the treatment option when it was offered.

We went into my office and spent a considerable time getting his breathing and anxiety under control as he was hyperventilating and was unable to regulate his responses or to verbalise what was going on. Eventually he began to settle down, and through silent tears, he informed me that he knew what was wrong with him and that he had to talk about it as he had avoided it for too long. He then informed me that he had been a happy working man and had never used drugs. He would go out with his mates and have a few pints but was a settled and stable young man until he went to watch a football match with his childhood friend at Hillsborough. He described the whole scene, now public knowledge, and how he ended up squeezed so tightly in the crush that he couldn't move his hands from his sides. He could hear screaming and cries for help but could do nothing to save himself or anyone else.

Helplessness.

He then described how he turned his head to say something to his friend who was squeezed up against him in the crush, but he got no response. He filled with even more panic at not being able to free his arms and he screamed out for someone to help. But everyone else was in the same position and many were also unconscious. He described the moment that he realised that his friend was in fact dead and had been kept standing upright by the crush, stood next to him but not breathing. At this point his tears erupted into a primal roar. A release of so much pain, held inside for so long. I did the only thing I felt I was able to do, and I held him and allowed him to weep. I wept with him as it was such an unexpected and overwhelming moment. Beyond his tears I could hear Xmas carols and laughter coming from the rest of the building, but inside that room, we were caught in a moment in time which had completely changed a life.

After sobbing uncontrollably for a considerable time, he regained his composure and continued to talk. He said that eventually people were able to move onto the pitch and he was able to help carry his friend on to the field where he was indeed pronounced dead and was eventually taken to a makeshift mortuary. David was in a daze at that point and said that he was just wandering around the scene aimlessly. Then he remembered being outside of the stadium, with all of the chaos that was happening, and he began to walk alone, shocked, puzzled and grief stricken.

This was the tipping point for David. He did not know what to do, how to deal with what had just happened. In a few hours, his life had been destroyed. Everything had changed. How does a person, left alone and dazed after such an experience, come back from that? He walked and walked and was eventually approached by someone selling drugs.

He went with the guy to a flat and took heroin, initially smoked from the foil but very soon injected. It made the pain go away. It numbed him. He could cope. From that day he had used heroin daily. Ten years of avoiding that day, until the crowd of Xmas visitors triggered the panic attack, which resulted in that massive disclosure.

I felt very honoured to be the witness to such a personally traumatic disclosure. To have been able to hold the space and enable it to happen. To have been trusted in that moment. It was heart-warming to then witness his progress through treatment; to see his self-confidence grow without drugs, to see him leave, after several weeks, drug free and with the chance of a future.

I guess the moral of the story is 'Never judge a book by its cover'. You never know what has brought a person to where they are in life, whether they are unemployed, homeless or addicted. Every one of them has a story, and if you take the time to listen to that story, you might just understand them a bit better. I saw this on many occasions in Barley Wood. Often, I saw people who were judged harshly for stealing or who were forced into sex-work to feed their addictions, but every single one of them had a powerful story to back up why they ended up doing what they were doing. Nobody goes to a party at age eighteen and decides to become an addict. There is a progression and a deterioration of circumstances and opportunity which forces people into situations which they would never have contemplated even a short time before.

I was facilitating a group one morning in Barley Wood. The group I was taking were quite well-established, but a new lady called Carol had recently joined the group and was having difficulty acknowledging the severity of her addiction. She was around thirty-eight years old and lived alone with her almost four year old daughter. No matter what people shared in the group she did not identify. She insisted that no matter how her heroin addiction affected her, it had no impact on her child, who despite everything was clean, well fed and had all of her needs met. There was also a young man in the group called Brian who started to get angry at her rebuttal of every probable consequence. "You look a bit upset Brian," I said. "Is there something you would like to say to Carol?" Brian took a few deep breaths and shared an event which had finally forced him to step forward and ask for help. He described looking after his three year old son whilst he was using heroin. He said his son was OK. But he had taken heroin and fallen asleep on the couch. Meanwhile, his son had moved a stool, climbed up and got his dad's methadone from the top of the fridge freezer as he had witnessed his dad doing many times. He unscrewed the lid and drunk a large amount of the sweet-tasting green liquid. When his dad woke up, he was lying unconscious on the kitchen floor and had to be rushed to hospital where he narrowly avoided death. By the time he finished the story he was very tearful and upset as was Carol who was finally reached by the honesty of another.

She then described, in detail, an event which had happened shortly before coming into treatment. She lived in a flat in London where the toilet was accessed via the kitchen, and when she needed to inject heroin in her groin, she would sit on the side of the bath whilst she did so and keep an eye on her daughter playing on the kitchen floor. She described the timeline of events until she injected and she 'went over' falling to the floor unconscious. She then described waking up feeling confused because she was sitting up with her back against the bath, her jeans and underwear were pulled up and fastened, the used needle was back in its sheath and her daughter was holding her hand, saying, "Come on, Mummy, come on!" At that moment the group descended into floods of tears at the power of the disclosure and Carol crossed the circle to hug and thank Brian for his honesty. Moments like this were so powerful and so effective in getting people to feel supported in a situation which feels so very shameful. How else could we ever heal if we were so ashamed to ask for help or support.

My experience of working within this busy facility was amazing and grounding in how to work with a large number of complex clients, in a very stressful environment, but still see positive change happening for many people. It was the springboard for me to become brave enough to change and develop the rigid treatment models which were used to treat addictions. Without this foundation I would not have had the courage to eventually do it alone and believe in myself.

In conclusion, this snapshot of my life does not really even scratch the surface of some of the experiences I have lived through, they are merely examples of what I was forced to look at during one episode of my life in 1996. This year will be my twenty-sixth year in recovery from addiction and I haven't addressed any of that here, what happened after I left Barley Wood, and what the differences are in living life on life's terms; without alcohol or drugs to soften the blow. One of the best definitions of addiction I ever heard was in an early AA meeting in Loughton, Essex whilst I was waiting to get into rehab. An elderly gentleman shared, very eloquently about his drinking and how he managed to stop through coming to AA. He said that he didn't really understand the Steps but that repeating 'Just for Today' was enough to keep him sober on a daily basis. He then said, "I don't know how to describe alcoholism as I'm not a professional, but I always felt like I had a layer of skin missing, therefore everything hurt me." This still touches me in its simplicity and honesty.

Below is a brief overview of my twelve-step treatment experience. The first five Steps:

Step One

We admitted we were powerless over our addiction, that our lives had become unmanageable.

The majority of the dialogue in my book is primarily Step One: Examples and evidence that my addiction was out of control and was causing me major distress. The unmanageability is referring to every aspect of one's life which begins to 'unravel' and cause ever increasing emotional and physical pain, which in turn needs ever increasing levels of sedation in order to keep it at bay until it can no longer be kept at bay, no matter how much we try.

Although I believe that trauma underpins most addictive behaviours, it is the progressive nature of addiction which creates the ever-increasing pain. Drugs and alcohol work initially, but very soon become the very thing which makes everything worse. They eventually lead to complete isolation so our disordered thought processes become even more self-destructive because they tell us there is no way out.

Step One is the foundation stone for long term recovery. If we cannot be fully honest about what happened in the darkest days of our addiction, we are in grave danger of repeating the patterns which caused us so much pain. Denial is often referred to as a factor which is indeed true, but denial does not gain any strength or impetus if we have a strong step one.

Denial is there for a purpose. It helps us to get through

difficult experiences such as grief and loss. Denial keeps us safe in the middle of a physical or emotional event which may be overwhelming and then eventually we try to let go and forget or we begin to minimise how traumatic an event was. Many women talk of denial being a major part in allowing themselves to become pregnant again, as they forget how overwhelming and traumatic the whole experience may have been for them. This is healthy denial as it allows procreation to continue despite the risks and pain involved.

Step One is about blocking that denial by keeping a clear record of what we did and how we felt, who we hurt and the shame we created. If this is not allowed to be 'archived and forgotten' then denial cannot take hold. Step One is the evidence that we cannot safely engage with certain substances or behaviours.

Almost a quarter of a century after I had my last drink, when I am struggling with low mood, or I am grieving or feeling angry or distressed, my body still suggests a drink might help, and without my step one 'evidence' in my body and mind, I may well have allowed myself to believe that I could manage 'just one' when I know for sure that it was never possible for me to simply have one. Never.

Make sure that your step one has everything that you can possibly remember. Do it well, then do it again because you will remember something new. Sceptics say that it is dwelling in the past and allowing old behaviours to make us feel shame and guilt. I say to them, 'No'; it is the key to begin to release guilt and shame and to forgive ourselves for the terrible situations we found ourselves in and the negative way in which we managed them. I no longer carry shame and guilt about my past or I could never have shared my personal story.

My guilt and shame are evident on every page of my story because that is how I lived my life in addiction, but now I can measure the change and growth I have made over the years. I may well be far away from my last drink, but without my recovery programme I could be very close to my next drink.

Step Two

We came to believe that a power greater than ourselves could restore us to sanity.

Although written over seventy-five years ago in the US Bible Belt, this step does not mean that we have to 'find God'. Though back then, it was very relevant in that part of the world. Nowadays, across the world in multicultural and secular communities, the twelve-step programme is successfully working to keep people in recovery from addiction. A power greater than ourselves can mean whatever it means for an individual. For some it is AA or NA, the power of a group of people who are already living alcohol and drug free lives. It can be an individual who inspires us to do better or a deceased relative whom we feel is watching over us and wanting the best for us. For many people it is God, but not necessarily religion, which is often seen as a man-made construct. I have probably met thousands of people in the last days of their addictions and "Dear God, please help me" is not an uncommon cry when the daily agony becomes unbearable. For some people this can lead to a spiritual awakening when the body and mind begin to feel better, and confidence and self-esteem grow. We feel grateful that we have been given another opportunity at life so we thank the God that we cried out for in despair.

For many people, particularly those from oppressive and abusive childhoods, God is often the focus of the anger and despair. "Why did he do this to me? Why did he allow all those terrible things to happen to me? There's no God caring for or protecting me." I myself tried to sit in AA meetings, before finding recovery, and had to leave because I could see and hear the word 'God' being banded around and it made me angry and rageful, because I was looking to blame everything *outside of myself* rather than take any responsibility *for myself*. When I finally understood that Step Two was actually about me reaching out and connecting with others, asking for help, acknowledging that I could not do this alone and that I needed support, it made perfect sense. In treatment I connected with my peers, my counsellors and maybe for the first time ever, I felt safe and understood. My inner critic became less intrusive in my thoughts and I started to ignore it more and listen to others instead of believing all of the lies which my own thoughts kept telling me. I did begin to believe that I wasn't bad or mad but was unwell and could heal.

Step Three

Made a decision to turn our will and our lives over to the care of God as we understood him.

When I finally understood this step, it was a revelation for me. Again, it isn't about God, it is about letting go of control and handing over some of the situations we find ourselves in and not becoming obsessed about controlling outcomes. The best example in my book is my attempts to find accommodation prior to leaving treatment. My self-will and ego were determined that

I was going to live in Bath, but despite spending several days trying to acquire an apartment, it clearly was not happening. Stubbornly, I intended returning until I found somewhere suitable, but my counsellor said, "Maybe you need to think about why this plan isn't working? Maybe your higher power has a better plan?"

I was perplexed by this and said, "What do you mean? I am putting all of my efforts into getting somewhere."

"Yes," he replied, "but you've put such tight parameters on your search, and it is bearing no fruit, so maybe you need to widen your scope." As described in the book, I decided to try Weston and found a deposit bond and a beautiful apartment within half an hour. This simplicity suddenly made so much sense and Step Three continues to be my favourite step. Whenever I feel I am getting nowhere, or I am stressing about possible outcomes, I ensure I have done everything that I can do, and I hand it over to the universe and whatever happens is meant to be. This saves an unbelievable amount of stress, worry and turmoil for me and I am now quite adept at accepting the outcome, whether good or bad.

Steps Four and Five

4. Made a searching and fearless moral inventory of ourselves.

5. Admitted to God, to ourselves and to another human being the exact nature of our wrongs.

These two steps go hand in hand and are a very powerful combination in addiction recovery. As with Step One, we must dig deep and be 'fearless and searching' in our moral inventory.

Who have I hurt? How has my behaviour affected those around me? When have I lied? We go through our whole lives and try to identify repeating behaviours; anger, resentment, aggression, jealousy, rage and we write them all down. When, how, who and what happened. It is a huge piece of work, and it generates a tsunami of guilt and shame which subsequently must be managed, but it is cathartic and healthy.

The second part, Step Five, is to read the content to another human being, often to a sponsor or fellowship member. Although terrifying, this is a way to begin releasing the shame and guilt by saying it out loud and letting someone else know your deepest and darkest secrets. The feeling of 'release' when we finally say it out loud and hear it in someone's presence is an unbelievable feeling and, as a lapsed Catholic, it taught me what the concept of confession was all about. It wasn't about God punishing and giving penance, it is about unburdening ourselves. I argued with priests for many years and refused to go to confession as I couldn't accept that God had forgiven me, yet on judgement day, I had to answer again for all my sins? Where is the forgiveness in that teaching?

Suddenly, in a rehab clinic, facing an old grey-haired lady wearing a twinset and pearls, I told my truth which I feared would shock her but she didn't flinch, and I felt the benefit immediately. I cried with the relief, and she simply sat in silence until I stopped. She then looked at me, smiled and gently said, "Shall we say the serenity prayer?" It was simply a deep confession without all the dogma of organised religion and her calmness and lack of judgement helped me to increase my trust in the twelve-step process.

When we make ourselves vulnerable and humble, not asking for material wealth but asking for the help and strength that we need to make us better human beings, there is an energetic shift which takes place and which opens us up to accepting positive and healing energy. We are unable to accept this energy until we have done sufficient honest work on ourselves, because we cannot see or feel the energy when we are blinded by feelings such as rage, anger and shame.

Again, as a Catholic, I struggled with the concept of 'Jesus' being a saintly white European with a bleeding heart and holes in his hands, but my life changed for the better almost immediately when I reached out to my sister for help. I began to believe, in the early days when I still felt suicidal, that maybe there *was* a plan for my life. That maybe I *was* worth fighting for. That maybe I *didn't* have the power or skills to run my life single-handedly; I needed to connect with others and *accept their help*, however it looked or felt.

It wasn't too long before I started to feel the benefits of this and began to believe that some spiritual entity was indeed available to me and gave me hope and strength. I used the word God but visualised deceased family members or a universal life-force. I started to pray but not in a religious format; I asked for guidance, wisdom, hope and strength every day. I asked that I be honest and open-minded in all my communications, and I asked daily that I should not pick up a drink or drug. I began to find reflective time extremely beneficial and, for the first time ever, I began to enjoy my own company rather than my lifetime of 'looking for fun'.

Just for Today (Courtesy of Alcoholics Anonymous)

Just for today, I will try to live through this day only, and not tackle all my problems at once. I can do something for twelve hours that would appal me if I felt that I had to keep it up for a lifetime.

- Just for today I will be happy. This assumes what Abraham Lincoln says to be true; that most folks are as happy as they make up their minds to be.

- Just for today I will adjust myself to what is, and not try to adjust everything to my own desires. I will take my luck as it comes and fit myself to it.

- Just for today I will try to strengthen my mind. I will study. I will learn something useful. I will not be a mental loafer. I will read something that requires effort, thought and concentration.

- Just for today I will exercise my soul in three ways: I will do somebody a good turn, and not get found out; if anybody knows of it, it will not count. I will do at least two things I don't want to do just for exercise. I will not show anyone that my feelings are hurt; they may be hurt, but today I will not show it.

- Just for today I will be agreeable. I will look as well as I can, dress becomingly, keep my voice low, be courteous, criticise not one bit. I won't find fault with anything, nor try to improve or regulate anybody but myself.

- Just for today I will have a programme. I may not follow it exactly, but I will have it. I will save myself from two pests: hurry and indecision.

- Just for today I will have a quiet half hour all by myself and relax. During this half hour, I will try to get a better perspective of my life.

- Just for today I will be unafraid. I will not be afraid to enjoy what is beautiful and to believe that as I give to the world, so the world will give to me.

I would like to take this opportunity to thank every single person, good and bad, for coming into my life and teaching me lessons which I needed to learn. Thank you to all my friends and family whose support has been loyal and unswerving throughout my recovery. Thank you to the many professionals, sponsors, counsellors and supervisors who have supported me in my journey and finally thank you to the anonymous recovery fellowships, particularly AA, NA and CODA who have been there for me, all over the world, wherever I have travelled.

I will continue to write my truth, in the hope that someone else finds it interesting or funny or helpful and that it may shine a light for someone who is at a crossroads in their life and feels like there is no way out.

There is always a way out. It may not be easy, and it may involve having to reach out and ask for help, but it may be the most important thing that you ever do. Like me, asking for help can be the catalyst which changes absolutely everything, but you will never know if you don't ask.

Pick up the phone and talk to someone.

—Mike Delaney